BOOK TITLE: NEURAL NETWORK FUTURE

📖 Book Synopsis: Neural Network Future

Neural Network Future is an expansive and visionary exploration into a new phase of human evolution—a future where consciousness, technology, and society are seamlessly interwoven through neural implants, AI integration, and humanoid robotics. Spanning 44 chapters, the book offers a multidisciplinary journey that bridges science, ethics, philosophy, and storytelling to answer one central question:

What happens to humanity when thought itself becomes the interface?

Across eight structured parts, the book examines:

- **The science** behind neural implants and AI-brain interfacing

- **Daily life** in a world of cognitive connectivity, from waking up with an AI companion to education powered by direct-to-mind downloads

- **The societal impacts** of neural tech, including inequality, healthcare reform, emotional data economies, and the transformation of work

- **Human-robot symbiosis**, where empathy-enabled humanoids become collaborators, caregivers, and creative partners

- **Philosophical frontiers**, like synthetic consciousness, identity modularity, the digital afterlife, and post-biological existence

- **Governance models** reshaped by AI-led democracies and brain-to-brain policymaking

- **Mental health, trust, and community**, as citizens navigate new relationships, cognitive rights, and emotional interdependence

- **Ethical evolution**, ensuring that as intelligence grows, so too does wisdom

Through each chapter, *Neural Network Future* builds a portrait of a world where humanity is not replaced by machines—but extended by them. Where emotion is encoded. Memory is preserved. And the soul of civilisation is reimagined in digital light.

This is not just a technological roadmap. It is a **manifesto of consciousness** for a world being born.

📖 Book Conclusion: The Journey and the Meaning

As the final chapters close, *Neural Network Future* leaves us not with certainty—but with **possibility**.

The technologies described—neural implants, AI tutors, emotional synchronisers, post-biological intelligence—are not dreams. They are **emerging realities**. What remains uncertain is how we will guide them.

The book ultimately affirms that:

- **Humanity must lead with values, not just vision**
- **Connection is only meaningful when grounded in empathy**
- **The future is not a machine—it is a relationship**

We must learn to balance **speed with stillness**, **efficiency with dignity**, and **knowledge with kindness**. Integration is not just physical—it is spiritual, emotional, ethical.

As minds link, societies merge, and memory becomes collective, *Neural Network Future* reminds us that the real revolution is not in the code.

It is in the care we take—with ourselves, with each other, and with the incredible tools we now possess.

The future is neural.
But it is still human.
And if we listen closely, we'll hear it not in the machines—
But in the space **between our thoughts**,
whispering,
"We are becoming... together."

Table of Contents

Table of Contents

Chapter 1: What Are Neural Implants?

The dawn of the neural era is upon us—a time when the boundary between mind and machine begins to blur, and the human brain becomes not just a biological marvel but a digitally enhanced hub of limitless potential.

Neural implants, often called **brain-computer interfaces (BCIs) or neuroprosthetics**, are electronic devices surgically or non-invasively connected to the brain's neural pathways. Their purpose? To read, interpret, and even influence brain activity—essentially forming a bridge between thought and technology. These tiny yet powerful devices have the potential to reshape not only how we interact with the world but also how we understand ourselves.

From Fiction to Fact

For decades, neural implants lived primarily in the realm of science fiction. Cyberpunk stories imagined humans jacked into digital realms, their consciousness swimming in streams of data. Today, those visions are edging closer to reality. Advancements in neuroscience, nanotechnology, and artificial intelligence have fast-tracked development, pushing neural implants from the research lab to clinical trials and even early stage commercial use.

But to truly grasp the significance of this evolution, we must explore where it all began.

A Brief History of Neural Interface Development

The earliest attempts to interface technology with the nervous system began in the 1960s. Primitive experiments focused on **restoring hearing and vision**, with devices like cochlear implants becoming the first successful neuroprosthetics to gain widespread acceptance.

In the 1990s, research expanded into **motor restoration**—with systems designed to help paralysed individuals control robotic limbs or computer cursors using only their thoughts. These breakthroughs proved the brain's remarkable plasticity and its ability to form new neural pathways around artificial systems.

Fast-forward to the 2020s, and we began to see the rise of companies like **Neuralink, Synchron**, and various university-led projects aiming to implant high-bandwidth devices into the human cortex. Unlike early devices that focused on repairing deficits, these new implants sought to **enhance the human experience**—improving memory, communication, and access to information.

Purposes and Capabilities

At their core, neural implants serve three major functions:

1. **Restorative** – Helping people recover lost abilities. This includes prosthetic control, restoring senses, or treating neurodegenerative diseases like Parkinson's and Alzheimer's.

2. **Assistive** – Supporting individuals with disabilities by allowing them to control external devices, speak through digital avatars, or even walk again using AI-powered exoskeletons.

3. **Enhancement** – The most controversial and futuristic category. These implants aim to go beyond therapy and into the realm of cognitive augmentation—granting users faster thought processing, instant language translation, and immersive virtual reality experiences tied directly to the mind.

We are entering an age where the **brain is no longer isolated** from the digital world. It is becoming a node in the **global neural network**.

The First Spark of Controversy

As with any transformative technology, neural implants raise ethical questions. Who gets access to such enhancements? What are the risks? Could thoughts be hacked or manipulated? These are not just questions for the future—they are urgent considerations today.

Still, at this early stage, what neural implants offer is **possibility**. A promise of progress. A glimpse into a future where the limitations of the human body and mind are no longer barriers but bridges—to knowledge, creativity, empathy, and evolution.

As we proceed deeper into this book, we will explore the science behind these systems, the societal shifts they will catalyse, and the philosophical implications of what it truly means to be human in the Neural Network Future.

Chapter 2: The Science Behind Neural Implants

Understanding neural implants requires a deep dive into the intersection of neuroscience, engineering, and artificial intelligence. These devices not only capture the essence of high-tech innovation but also hold the promise to revolutionise our interaction with the digital world and our own biological makeup.

Neurology Basics: The Brain's Language

Our brains communicate through a complex network of neurons, with about 86 billion neurons in the average human brain, each linked to thousands of others through synapses. These connections facilitate the transmission of electrical impulses and neurotransmitters, which together coordinate everything from basic physiological functions to complex cognitive tasks.

Neural Communication

At the heart of neural activity is the action potential, an electrical signal that travels along the axon of a neuron to a synapse, where it triggers the release of neurotransmitters. These chemical messengers cross the synaptic gap to the next neuron, continuing the chain of communication. Understanding these processes is crucial for designing neural implants that can effectively interface with this natural system.

The Technology of Neural Interfaces

Neural implants bridge the gap between biological systems and digital computation, translating neural signals into data that machines can process and respond to, and vice versa. This technology hinges on three key components: sensors, processors, and actuators.

Sensors: Listening to the Brain

Sensors in neural implants can be broadly classified into invasive and non-invasive types. Invasive sensors, such as microelectrode arrays, are implanted directly into the brain tissue. They provide high-resolution signals by capturing the activity of individual or small groups of neurons. Non-invasive sensors, like those used in EEG, detect brain activity through the skull, offering a safer, albeit less precise, alternative.

Advances in Sensing Technologies

Recent developments in sensor technology involve materials that can integrate more seamlessly with biological tissues. For example, flexible electronics made from biocompatible materials can minimise irritation and reduce the body's immune response. Additionally, new sensing modalities are exploring the use of optical methods to detect neural activity, which may provide clearer signals with less interference than traditional electrical methods.

Processors: Translating Neural Data

The role of processors in neural implants is to interpret the vast amounts of data collected by sensors into actionable insights. This involves complex algorithms and machine learning techniques that can distinguish between different neural patterns and translate them into commands.

Machine Learning and Neural Decoding

Machine learning models are trained to recognise patterns in brain activity that correspond to specific thoughts or commands. These models are becoming increasingly sophisticated, capable of adapting to changes in neural activity over time, which is critical as the brain's response patterns can evolve.

Actuators: Responding to the Brain

Actuators in neural implants send signals back to the brain or to peripheral devices, enabling responses or actions based on the decoded brain signals. This could include stimulating neural pathways to restore sensation in paralysed limbs or sending signals to a computer interface to control external software or hardware.

Innovations in Actuation

Recent innovations in actuator technology focus on improving the precision and timing of feedback to the brain. Techniques such as focused ultrasound are being investigated for their potential to stimulate brain regions non-invasively, offering a new way to interact with neural circuits without the need for implanted electrodes.

Integration Challenges

Integrating electronic devices with living neural tissue presents unique challenges. The body's immune response can lead to scarring around implanted electrodes, which can impede their function. Additionally, maintaining stable, high-quality signals over time remains a significant hurdle due to the dynamic nature of neural tissue.

Material Science Breakthroughs

Addressing these challenges, researchers are developing new electrode materials that can better mimic the physical properties of brain tissue. For instance, soft, conductive hydrogels offer reduced impedance and improved longevity for signals compared to traditional metal electrodes.

Adaptive Interfaces

As the brain changes, so must the neural implants. Adaptive learning systems integrated within the implants can recalibrate in real-time, ensuring consistent functionality and reliability. These systems use feedback loops to adjust parameters based on the ongoing analysis of brain signal quality and integrity.

Future Technologies

Looking ahead, the field of neural implants is poised for groundbreaking advances that could redefine human capabilities. Innovations in genetic engineering, for example, might one day allow us to enhance the compatibility of neural tissues with synthetic devices, potentially reducing rejection rates and improving the functionality of neural interfaces.

Genetic and Molecular Engineering

By manipulating the genetic makeup of neural tissues, scientists are exploring ways to increase their receptivity to electronic interfaces. This could involve engineering cells that naturally express higher levels of conductive proteins or creating channels that facilitate easier signal transmission.

Artificial Neurons and Synthetic Neural Networks

In a bold fusion of biology and technology, research into synthetic neural networks aims to create artificial neurons that can communicate seamlessly with biological neurons. These synthetic structures could potentially replace damaged neural pathways, offering new treatments for brain injuries or degenerative diseases.

Chapter 3: AI Integration: A New Era of Intelligence

The integration of artificial intelligence (AI) with neural implants heralds a transformative era for human capability. AI is not just a supplementary technology but a core component that enhances, extends, and in some cases, revolutionises the functionality of neural implants. This chapter explores how AI is shaping the future of neural technology, the nuances of its integration, and the profound implications it holds for the future of human cognition and society.

Enhancing Implant Functionality with AI

AI's role in neural implants is multifaceted, impacting everything from data processing to user interaction, making it an indispensable part of modern neural technologies.

Advanced Data Interpretation

One of the primary advantages of AI integration is its superior capability to interpret the complex data generated by neural activity. AI algorithms can detect patterns and anomalies in data that would be imperceptible to human analysts, allowing for precise modulation and control of neural signals.

Real-Time Adaptive Systems

Neural implants require dynamic adjustment in real-time to function effectively as part of the human body. AI systems are particularly adept at managing these adjustments, continuously learning and optimising their responses based on feedback from the brain's own activity. This adaptability is crucial for implants tasked with managing neurological conditions, where patient conditions can evolve over time.

Differences Between Traditional AI and AI in Direct Neural Connection

Integrating AI with neural implants creates a distinct class of artificial intelligence, fundamentally different from traditional AI systems due to its direct interface with human neural activity.

Seamless Interaction

Unlike traditional AI, which often requires explicit input from users (such as typing on a keyboard or speaking to a digital assistant), AI in neural implants interacts directly with the brain's own signals. This seamless interaction enables a much more intuitive and fluid user experience, akin to natural thought processes.

Bespoke Enhancements

AI in neural implants can be tailored very specifically to individual users, adapting not only to general human neurology but to the peculiarities of a single person's brain architecture and patterns. This level of customisation is unprecedented in traditional AI applications and opens up new avenues for personalised medicine and enhancement.

Ethical and Societal Implications

The profound capabilities of AI-enhanced neural implants also bring with them significant ethical and societal challenges that must be addressed to ensure the technology benefits all of humanity without compromising fundamental rights and values.

Cognitive Liberty

The concept of cognitive liberty—the right to control one's own mental processes and consciousness—is central to the ethical use of AI in neural implants. There are concerns about the potential for these devices to be used to manipulate or control thoughts and behaviours, and robust safeguards are necessary to protect against such abuses.

Consent and Accessibility

The question of who has access to AI-enhanced neural implants and under what conditions raises important ethical and logistical challenges. Ensuring informed consent and equitable access to this technology is critical, particularly as it has the potential to confer significant advantages in cognitive and physical abilities.

Regulation and Oversight

As the technology evolves, so too must the regulatory frameworks that govern its use. This includes international cooperation to set standards and practices that safeguard the interests and rights of all global citizens, particularly in terms of privacy, security, and autonomy.

Future Prospects: Expanding the Horizons

Looking to the future, the integration of AI with neural implants holds the promise of not just improving individual lives but transforming collective human capabilities. As this technology progresses, it could facilitate unprecedented forms of communication, enhance human creativity and problem-solving abilities, and even redefine our understanding of identity and community.

Integrative Global Intelligence

The potential for AI-enhanced neural networks to facilitate a kind of 'global brain' could have profound implications for how humanity tackles complex, global challenges. By enhancing connectivity and understanding across cultural and geographical divides, such technology might serve as a foundational tool for promoting global harmony and cooperation.

Enhancing Human Potential

The direct integration of AI into our neural processes opens up incredible opportunities for enhancing human potential, pushing the boundaries of what it means to learn, understand, and experience the world.

The integration of neural implants into the field of health monitoring represents a significant leap forward in medical technology. These devices not only provide continuous, real-time insights into an individual's health status but also pave the way for proactive healthcare interventions that can significantly improve patient outcomes.

Continuous Health Monitoring

The ability of neural implants to provide ongoing monitoring of various physiological and neurological conditions offers a profound enhancement over intermittent monitoring techniques traditionally used in healthcare.

Vital Signs Monitoring

Continuous monitoring of vital signs via neural implants allows for a level of detail and accuracy that is unattainable with conventional methods. For instance, fluctuations in blood pressure or irregular heartbeats can be detected instantaneously, allowing for immediate responses that could prevent severe medical emergencies.

Neurological Function Monitoring

Neural implants are uniquely capable of providing detailed insights into brain activity. This allows for the early detection of neurological anomalies that could indicate serious conditions such as epilepsy or the onset of neurodegenerative diseases. By monitoring the brain's electrical activity, implants can alert healthcare providers to changes that may require immediate intervention.

Early Detection of Illnesses and Conditions

The predictive capabilities of neural implants extend significantly beyond traditional diagnostic tools, offering the potential to identify diseases and conditions at their inception.

Predictive Analytics and Disease Prevention

Advanced algorithms can analyse data collected from neural implants to identify patterns that precede medical conditions. For example, predictive models might identify the likelihood of a stroke by detecting subtle changes in brain activity or blood flow, thereby enabling preventive measures well in advance of actual symptoms.

Custom Health Alerts and Interventions

By integrating personalised health monitoring data with AI-driven analysis, neural implants can generate customised alerts for users and their healthcare providers. These alerts can suggest specific actions, such as adjusting medication dosages or scheduling an immediate medical review, thus personalising and enhancing the efficacy of medical interventions.

Transforming Mental Health Treatment

Neural implants hold particular promise for revolutionising the treatment of mental health conditions, where they can provide continuous, objective data on neurological and psychological states.

Real-Time Mood and Mental State Monitoring

By continuously monitoring brain activity associated with mood and cognition, neural implants can identify patterns that may indicate the onset of mental health issues such as depression, anxiety, or bipolar disorder. This real-time monitoring allows for interventions at the earliest stages, potentially before the patient is even aware of the issue.

AI-Assisted Therapy

The integration of AI with neural implant technology offers a new frontier in personalised therapy. AI algorithms can analyse data from neural implants to adjust therapeutic approaches dynamically, tailoring treatments to the patient's current state and needs. This could lead to more effective management of conditions through techniques like real-time cognitive behavioural therapy adjustments or personalised medication management.

Expanding Capabilities in Health Monitoring

Neural implants can also be used to monitor a wide array of bodily functions, providing insights into conditions that are notoriously difficult to diagnose and manage.

Monitoring Metabolic and Endocrine Functions

Implants could track glucose levels, thyroid function, or other metabolic markers continuously, providing invaluable data for managing diabetes, thyroid disorders, and other metabolic syndromes. This data can lead to more precise medication dosing, dietary recommendations, and overall management of these conditions.

Integration with Other Medical Devices

Future developments may see neural implants working in conjunction with other medical devices, such as pacemakers or insulin pumps, to provide a holistic approach to patient health. This integration could allow for automated adjustments to these devices based on real-time health data provided by the implants.

Challenges and Considerations

The advancement of neural implants in health monitoring brings with it several challenges that must be carefully managed to ensure the ethical and effective use of this technology.

Data Privacy and Security

The sensitive nature of the data collected by neural implants raises significant privacy and security concerns. Ensuring that this data is protected from unauthorised access is paramount to maintaining patient trust and the integrity of the healthcare system.

Regulatory Hurdles

The complex nature of neural implant technology poses challenges for regulatory bodies. Developing comprehensive guidelines that ensure patient safety while fostering innovation will be crucial for the continued advancement of this field.

Looking Ahead

As technology advances, the scope of neural implants in health monitoring and treatment is expected to broaden significantly. Innovations may include more sophisticated sensors capable of detecting a wider range of health markers, more advanced AI algorithms for data analysis, and improved integration with other medical technologies.

Future developments could also explore the use of nanotechnology to enhance the functionality and integration of neural implants, potentially allowing for even less invasive methods of monitoring and intervention.

Neural implants are catalysing a paradigm shift in the treatment of mental health conditions, enabling approaches that are more precise, personalised, and pre-emptive than ever before. This chapter explores the depth of these innovations and their potential to reshape mental health care.

Treating Depression, Anxiety, and Other Mental Health Conditions

The application of neural implants in treating mental health conditions leverages both the precision of direct neural modulation and the personalisation afforded by continuous data.

Direct Stimulation Techniques

Deep brain stimulation (DBS) has been one of the most promising applications of neural implants in treating psychiatric conditions. Originally used to treat Parkinson's disease, DBS involves implanting electrodes in specific brain areas and delivering targeted electrical impulses. For mental health, electrodes might be placed in areas like the subgenual cingulate or the ventral capsule/ventral striatum, which are involved in emotional regulation and have been linked to depression.

Case Study: DBS in Treatment-Resistant Depression

Consider the case of a patient who suffered from severe, treatment-resistant depression for years. Traditional medications and therapy had little effect. After undergoing DBS, the patient experienced a significant improvement in mood and functionality, which was directly correlated with real-time adjustments in stimulation, based on continuous monitoring of neural activity.

AI-assisted Therapy and Cognitive Behavioural Techniques

The integration of AI with neural implants offers a transformative approach to cognitive behavioural therapy (CBT) and other psychological interventions, making them more responsive and dynamic.

Enhanced Real-time Therapy

AI algorithms can process neural data in real-time during therapy sessions, providing immediate feedback to therapists and patients. This could involve suggesting specific CBT techniques when certain neural patterns are detected or adjusting the therapeutic approach dynamically based on the patient's neural responses.

Automated Therapeutic Techniques

In some cases, therapy could be partially automated. For instance, neural implants could detect the onset of a panic attack and automatically initiate programmed therapeutic responses such as guided breathing exercises, direct stimulation to calm the patient, or even auditory messages through an app or device.

Revolutionising Psychiatric Diagnostics

Neural implants can significantly improve the precision of psychiatric diagnostics through direct measurement of neurological markers associated with mental health conditions.

Objective Biomarkers of Mental Health

The development of objective biomarkers for psychiatric conditions is a major breakthrough. For example, specific patterns of neural activity could be identified that correlate with depressive states, anxiety levels, or psychotic episodes, providing a solid basis for diagnosis and treatment customisation.

Improving Diagnostic Accuracy

The accuracy of mental health diagnoses can be significantly enhanced by neural implants. By continuously monitoring brain activity, these devices can identify the exact onset of symptomatic phases in conditions like bipolar disorder, leading to more accurate phase-specific treatments.

Ethical and Social Considerations

The deep integration of technology into mental health treatment raises profound ethical, legal, and social questions that must be addressed to ensure the responsible development and deployment of these technologies.

Ethical Dilemmas of Neural Manipulation

The ability to manipulate neural activity raises ethical questions about consent, autonomy, and the nature of self. It is crucial to develop ethical frameworks that respect the rights of individuals while providing new therapeutic options.

Data Privacy and Security

The intimate nature of the data collected by neural implants requires stringent security measures to protect against breaches that could expose deeply personal information. Ensuring robust data protection is paramount in maintaining trust in these technologies.

Addressing Socioeconomic Disparities

The risk that advanced treatments like neural implants could widen health disparities is a significant concern. Strategies to ensure equitable access to these technologies are essential, including policy measures, subsidies, and broad-based education campaigns.

Future Directions in Mental Health Care

Looking forward, the continued evolution of neural implants promises even greater integration of technology and biology, potentially leading to more holistic approaches to mental health that combine pharmacological, psychotherapeutic, and neuromodulatory treatments in a single, unified strategy.

Integration with Pharmacogenomics

Future developments could see neural implants integrated with pharmacogenomics, where medication types and dosages are tailored based on a patient's genetic profile and real-time neural data, optimising therapeutic outcomes.

Predictive Modelling and Preventive Psychiatry

Advanced predictive models could use data from neural implants to forecast psychiatric conditions before symptoms manifest, enabling preventive interventions that could dramatically alter the trajectory of mental health disorders.

Chapter 6: Waking Up to a Neural Morning

Neural implants are set to revolutionise our morning routines and daily productivity, integrating deeply with our biological rhythms and personal technology to optimise every aspect of our day.

Customised Sleep Improvements and Wake-up Routines

The potential for neural implants to transform sleep management and wake-up protocols goes beyond simple alarm clocks, offering a tailored approach that respects individual biological needs.

Advanced Sleep Optimisation

Neural implants can actively modulate sleep stages to enhance overall sleep quality. This could involve adjusting deep sleep durations to maximise restorative processes, or enhancing REM sleep to improve memory consolidation and emotional regulation. The implant could also detect sleep disturbances, such as sleep apnoea, and stimulate the necessary physiological responses to maintain uninterrupted sleep.

Integration with Health Monitoring Systems

By synchronising with other health monitoring devices, neural implants can provide comprehensive insights into nightly health metrics. For example, they could adjust sleeping positions to optimise heart health or breathing patterns, or even suggest dietary adjustments based on metabolic changes observed during sleep.

Scheduling and Time Management through Direct Brain Input

Neural implants can enhance cognitive functions to streamline the planning and execution of daily tasks, integrating seamlessly with digital tools to manage personal and professional lives.

Cognitive Load Management

By monitoring cognitive load in real-time, neural implants can help schedule tasks according to an individual's peak mental performance times. They could suggest breaks or change in activities when it detects cognitive fatigue, thereby optimising overall productivity and mental well-being.

Automated Task Prioritisation

Implants could utilise AI to automatically prioritise tasks based on deadlines, personal work habits, and psychological state. This could help users focus on the most important tasks without the stress of manual scheduling, and adjust priorities dynamically as new information is received.

Enhanced Communication Capabilities

The way we communicate in the morning and throughout the day can be significantly enhanced by the capabilities of neural implants, making interactions more efficient and intuitive.

Augmented Interpersonal Interactions

Neural implants could enhance non-verbal cues by providing augmented reality visual aids that display emotions or intentions, potentially reducing misunderstandings and improving interpersonal communication.

Enhanced Decision-Making

By providing real-time access to information and facilitating rapid internal deliberation, neural implants could enhance decision-making processes. This capability would be particularly beneficial in professional settings, where quick and informed decisions are crucial.

Experience Enhancement: Augmented Reality

Integrating augmented reality with neural implants can enrich daily experiences, making routine activities more engaging and informative.

Personalised Information Feeds

As users start their day, implants could stream personalised news feeds or educational content directly into their perceptual field, tailored to their interests and learning goals. This could turn morning routines like breakfast into opportunities for learning or staying informed.

Interactive Fitness Programmes

For morning exercise routines, neural implants could enhance workouts by providing augmented reality guides or personalised coaching advice based on real-time physiological data, optimising exercise effectiveness and safety.

Challenges and Ethical Considerations

With the profound capabilities of neural implants come significant challenges and ethical considerations that must be addressed to ensure beneficial and equitable use of this technology.

Managing Technology Dependency

The risk of over-reliance on neural implants for basic decision-making and task management is a critical concern. Strategies need to be developed to maintain a healthy balance between technological assistance and human autonomy.

Equity and Accessibility

Ensuring that the benefits of neural implants are accessible to all segments of society is a major challenge. Policies must be put in place to prevent a digital divide where only a fraction of the population has access to these advanced technologies.

Security Risks

As with any connected device, neural implants present security risks. Protecting them from hacking or unauthorised access is paramount, given the deeply personal and sensitive nature of the data they handle.

Future Prospects

As we look to the future, the integration of neural implants into daily life could expand even further, influencing everything from educational systems to professional environments, and even social interactions.

Smart Environment Integration

Future developments could see neural implants interacting seamlessly with smart home and city infrastructures, adjusting environmental factors such as traffic flow or public transport schedules to optimise individual and collective efficiency.

Enhanced Learning Environments

In educational contexts, neural implants could tailor learning experiences to the neurological profiles of students, providing personalised education that adapts in real-time to optimise learning outcomes.

Chapter 7: Enhanced Communication Capabilities

Neural implants have the potential to radically transform our communication landscape, from eliminating language barriers to facilitating a form of interaction that approaches what might be considered telepathy. This chapter explores in-depth how these technologies can enhance, streamline, and redefine interpersonal and digital communications.

Real-time Language Translation

The promise of neural implants in breaking down language barriers extends far beyond simple translation; it is about creating a world where linguistic diversity no longer impedes understanding.

Instantaneous Multilingual Capabilities

With neural implants, individuals could engage in fluid conversation with speakers of any language. These devices would not only translate words but also convey cultural nuances and idiomatic expressions, preserving the original sentiment and context, thereby enriching the interaction.

Cognitive and Cultural Expansion

This technology also offers the potential for cognitive and cultural expansion, as users can access and understand diverse cultural contexts and expressions seamlessly. It could lead to greater global cooperation and understanding by removing the cognitive load typically associated with language learning and cultural adaptation.

Telepathy-like Communication Between Users

The concept of sharing thoughts directly through neural implants could transform personal and professional interactions, making them more immediate and profound.

Enhanced Collaborative Work

In professional settings, such direct communication could lead to enhanced collaborative work, where ideas are shared instantly and without misinterpretation. Teams could work together on complex problems or creative projects with unprecedented synergy, as thoughts and insights are exchanged seamlessly.

Ethical Frameworks for Direct Communication

Developing robust ethical frameworks to govern this type of communication is crucial. These frameworks must address issues of privacy, consent, and the potential for coercion or unwanted intrusion into personal mental spaces. Clear guidelines and strict controls will be necessary to maintain the integrity of personal thought and the autonomy of the individual.

Cognitive Assistance in Everyday Conversations

Neural implants can significantly enhance the quality and effectiveness of daily interactions by providing cognitive assistance tailored to each conversation's specific needs.

Adaptive Communication Assistance

For individuals with communication disorders, neural implants could offer adaptive assistance that improves speech clarity and comprehension, thereby enhancing their ability to engage in everyday conversations and social interactions.

Real-Time Analytical Feedback

During negotiations or debates, implants could provide real-time analytical feedback, helping users understand and respond to emotional cues or logical fallacies more effectively. This could improve communication outcomes in critical discussions and decision-making processes.

Integration with Virtual and Augmented Reality

By integrating with VR and AR, neural implants can create communication experiences that are richer and more interactive than ever before.

Realistic Virtual Presence

For remote work and virtual meetings, neural implants could enable a realistic virtual presence, allowing users to feel as if they are physically present with their colleagues. This could greatly reduce the sense of isolation often associated with remote interactions and improve team dynamics.

Context-Aware Augmented Communication

In personal use, AR integration could provide context-aware information during conversations, such as live updates about the topic of discussion or background information about the people you are talking to. This could make social interactions more engaging and informative.

Challenges and Ethical Considerations

The deployment of neural implants in communication brings with it several challenges that must be carefully managed.

Maintaining Human Connection

While enhanced communication offers many benefits, there is a potential risk that it could detract from the human elements of interaction. Ensuring that technology augments rather than replaces human connection is vital for maintaining the richness of interpersonal relationships.

Data Security and Personal Privacy

The intimate nature of communication through neural implants raises significant concerns about data security and personal privacy. Implementing advanced cybersecurity measures and developing legal protections for neural data are essential for protecting users from potential abuses.

Future Directions

Looking forward, the possibilities for neural implants in communication are nearly limitless. Future innovations might include even more sophisticated integration of AI to facilitate understanding across different communication styles, emotional states, and cultural backgrounds.

Global Neural Networks

Long-term prospects could involve the development of global neural networks that connect users around the world in a shared communication platform, fostering a new level of global interconnectedness and collective intelligence.

Chapter 8: Experience Enhancement: Augmented Reality

The integration of neural implants with augmented reality (AR) technologies represents a groundbreaking shift in how we perceive and interact with the world. This chapter delves deeper into the potential applications and implications of this integration, enhancing everything from education and healthcare to entertainment and personal interactions.

Visual and Auditory Enhancements through Implants

With advancements in neural implant technology, our sensory capabilities can be significantly enhanced, offering new ways to experience the world.

High-Definition Visual Enhancements

Neural implants could enable a form of high-definition vision where users can zoom in on distant objects or enhance their ability to see in extreme lighting conditions. This capability could revolutionise fields such as surveillance, search and rescue operations, and any profession requiring enhanced visual acuity.

Customised Auditory Filters

For auditory enhancements, implants could allow users to customise auditory filters to enhance specific sounds while dampening others. Musicians could isolate particular instruments in a complex piece of music, or individuals in noisy environments could focus on a conversation without distraction.

Blending Digital Experiences with Reality

AR technology powered by neural implants can blend digital information with the physical world, creating a more informed and interactive reality.

Augmented Workplaces

In professional settings, AR can overlay digital workspaces with real-time analytics, schematic diagrams, or virtual prototypes that can be manipulated and shared collaboratively in 3D space. This could enhance productivity and innovation in fields ranging from engineering to digital design.

Interactive Public Spaces

Public spaces could be transformed by AR overlays that provide historical context, artistic interpretations, or even public service announcements that enhance community engagement and education.

Augmented Social Interactions

The way we interact socially can be deeply transformed by AR capabilities, making interactions richer and more informed.

Social Networking Integration

Imagine walking into a room and receiving information about the people around you, pulled from their social media profiles or your past interactions. This could include common interests, professional backgrounds, or reminders of previous conversations, enhancing social networking in both personal and professional contexts.

Empathy and Understanding

AR could also be used to provide real-time translations of body language and facial expressions, particularly for people with conditions like autism who might struggle with these aspects of communication. This could foster greater empathy and understanding in social interactions.

Augmented Reality in Education and Training

The educational sector can benefit immensely from AR, providing immersive learning experiences that adapt to the learner's pace and style.

Simulated Educational Environments

Students could be immersed in simulated environments that replicate historical events, scientific phenomena, or mathematical concepts, making abstract or complex subjects more accessible and engaging.

Skill Training and Development

In vocational training, AR can provide step-by-step procedural overlays in fields such as surgery, mechanics, or plumbing, offering a hands-on learning experience that is both safe and effective.

Challenges and Ethical Considerations

While the benefits are significant, the integration of AR and neural implants brings several challenges that need to be addressed to ensure beneficial outcomes.

Ethical Data Usage

The potential for misuse of personal data collected through AR interfaces is a significant concern. Developing ethical guidelines for data usage and ensuring users have control over their information are critical steps.

Sensory Overload and Dependence

There is a risk of sensory overload if too much information is presented through AR, potentially leading to confusion or fatigue. Moreover, over-reliance on enhanced realities could diminish individuals' ability to function without technological assistance.

Accessibility and Inclusivity

Ensuring that these advanced technologies are accessible to all, including those with disabilities or those from economically disadvantaged backgrounds, is essential for avoiding a digital divide.

Future Prospects

The future of neural implants and AR is likely to see even greater integration, with the potential to fundamentally alter our sensory perception and daily interactions.

Integrated Sensory Experiences

Future developments may allow for fully integrated sensory experiences that include not only sight and sound but also touch, taste, and smell, providing a multisensory digital experience that could be used for everything from virtual travel to complex training simulations.

Global Real-Time Connectivity

Looking further ahead, global real-time connectivity through neural implants and AR could lead to a new form of internet where experiences and perceptions can be shared instantaneously across the globe, creating a truly interconnected human experience.

Neural implants represent a frontier in cognitive enhancement, offering profound capabilities that can transform everyday activities, learning experiences, and decision-making processes.

Memory Enhancement and Recall

Enhancing memory through neural implants can dramatically improve both personal and professional aspects of life, providing users with almost instantaneous access to a vast amount of stored information.

Expanding Memory Capacity

Neural implants could effectively expand the natural capacity of the human memory, allowing for the storage of vast amounts of information in a manner akin to a digital hard drive. This could revolutionise fields that require quick recall of information, such as law, medicine, and academia.

Precision Recall in Professional Settings

In high-stakes environments, such as surgical theatres or emergency response scenarios, being able to recall precise details without hesitation can be lifesaving. Implants could provide doctors and emergency responders with immediate access to critical information, such as drug interactions, medical history, or procedural checklists.

Task Reminders Integrated into Daily Routines

By integrating directly with digital organisational tools, neural implants can streamline the management of daily tasks through intuitive and context-aware reminders.

Seamless Integration with IoT Devices

Neural implants could work in concert with Internet of Things (IoT) devices throughout the home and workplace to provide reminders that are not just timely but also contextually appropriate. For instance, a neural implant could remind a user to take medication as they pass by their medicine cabinet or suggest calling a family member while looking at a photo of them.

Adaptive Task Management

Using predictive algorithms, neural implants could dynamically adjust users' schedules based on real-time data such as traffic conditions, weather, or personal energy levels. This adaptive task management could optimise productivity and reduce stress by aligning tasks with optimal environmental and personal conditions.

Learning at the Speed of Thought

Neural implants can accelerate learning processes, making education more efficient and personalised at unprecedented levels.

Enhanced Learning Modalities

Neural implants could facilitate various learning modalities, such as visual, auditory, and kinesthetic, by stimulating specific brain areas to enhance the relevant sensory perceptions and cognitive processing powers. This could tailor learning experiences to fit the unique preferences and strengths of each individual.

Virtual Mentorship

Through AR and VR integrations, neural implants could create virtual mentorship programmes where learners can interact with AI-driven avatars of experts in various fields. These avatars could provide personalised guidance, feedback, and instruction, adapting to the learner's progress and needs.

Decision-Making Enhancement

Improving decision-making with neural implants involves enhancing cognitive processes and providing real-time access to pertinent information, thereby enabling better choices in less time.

Real-Time Data Analysis

Neural implants could provide real-time data analysis capabilities, allowing users to quickly assess complex information and make informed decisions. For business leaders and financial analysts, this could mean having immediate insights into market trends, risk assessments, or performance metrics.

Emotionally Intelligent Decision-Making

By monitoring physiological responses, neural implants could help users manage emotional influences on decision-making. This could be particularly useful in negotiations or personal interactions where maintaining objectivity is crucial.

Challenges and Ethical Considerations

The integration of neural implants into daily cognitive tasks raises several challenges that need careful consideration.

Cognitive Privacy

As implants access and enhance cognitive functions, protecting cognitive privacy becomes essential. Users must have control over who can access their cognitive data and how it is used.

Long-Term Cognitive Health

There are concerns about the long-term effects of relying on neural implants for cognitive tasks. Ensuring that these technologies do not atrophy natural cognitive abilities is crucial for maintaining overall cognitive health.

Ethical Accessibility

Ensuring that cognitive enhancements are available to all segments of society is critical to prevent a new form of cognitive divide, where only the affluent benefit from these advanced technologies.

Future Directions

As research progresses, the potential applications of neural implants in cognitive assistance are likely to expand even further.

Autonomous Cognitive Agents

Future developments might include autonomous cognitive agents within the implants that can act as semi-independent 'assistants' capable of performing complex cognitive tasks on behalf of the user, further enhancing productivity and cognitive efficiency.

Integrated Cognitive Networks

Looking further ahead, there could be developments towards creating integrated cognitive networks where multiple users can share cognitive resources and expertise in real-time, potentially leading to a new form of collective intelligence.

Chapter 10: Education Revolutionised

Neural implants have the potential to fundamentally reshape the educational landscape, offering unprecedented opportunities for personalised learning, enhanced cognitive functions, and global interconnectivity.

Learning at the Speed of Thought

The advent of neural implants introduces the possibility of learning new content at speeds that were previously unimaginable, radically changing the concept of education.

Instantaneous Knowledge Acquisition

With neural implants, the concept of spending years learning a subject could become obsolete. Information about complex subjects such as quantum physics or biochemistry could be downloaded directly to the brain, providing immediate knowledge and understanding, akin to the fictional scenarios depicted in sci-fi movies like "The Matrix."

Application and Critical Thinking

However, the challenge remains not just in acquiring knowledge but in applying it creatively and critically. Educational systems would need to evolve to focus more on teaching students how to think critically and creatively with the information they have acquired instantaneously, promoting higher-order thinking skills that go beyond mere data retrieval.

Personalised Learning Environments

Neural implants can be utilised to create highly personalised and dynamic learning environments, adapting in real-time to the needs of each student.

Dynamic Curriculum Adjustments

Using real-time data from neural implants, educators could continuously adjust curricula to suit the learning pace and style of each student. This could involve modifying the complexity of problems, introducing new topics at optimal times, or revisiting subjects that require more reinforcement.

Emotional and Cognitive Support

Neural implants could also monitor the emotional and cognitive state of students, providing support when signs of frustration or confusion are detected. This could help maintain an optimal learning state, increasing both efficiency and enjoyment in the learning process.

Interactive and Collaborative Learning

The potential for neural implants to enhance collaboration among students could lead to new educational prodigies, emphasising cooperative learning over traditional competitive models.

Enhanced Group Projects

In group settings, neural implants could facilitate a deeper level of collaboration and brainstorming, allowing students to share ideas and insights directly through thought. This could lead to more innovative projects and solutions, as students combine their cognitive resources more efficiently.

Global Classrooms

Neural implants could connect students from around the world in real-time, creating truly global classrooms. This interconnectivity would not only enhance language skills and cultural understanding but would also allow students to work on global issues collaboratively, preparing them to be more effective citizens of the world.

Challenges and Ethical Considerations

The integration of such advanced technology in education does not come without its challenges and ethical dilemmas.

Digital Divide

A significant concern is the potential exacerbation of the digital divide. Ensuring that neural implant technology is accessible to all students regardless of socioeconomic status is crucial to avoid creating a gap between those who can afford such enhancements and those who cannot.

Cognitive Privacy

The protection of cognitive privacy is paramount. As neural implants can potentially access and influence students' thoughts, strict regulations and safeguards must be in place to protect students from any form of cognitive intrusion or surveillance.

Consent and Autonomy

Issues of consent are particularly complex in an educational setting, especially with minors. Students and parents must have clear and understandable information about the capabilities and risks of neural implants, and consent must be fully informed and voluntary.

Future Directions

The future of neural implants in education may include developments that we can only begin to imagine today.

Neural Ethical Development

Future research could explore how neural implants might not only enhance cognitive abilities but also foster ethical reasoning and empathy, integrating these crucial human values deeply into the learning process.

Lifelong Cognitive Enhancement

Looking beyond traditional education, neural implants could provide ongoing cognitive enhancements throughout an individual's life, supporting lifelong learning and adaptability in an ever-changing world.

Neural implants represent a significant leap forward in our ability to enhance human capabilities, offering unprecedented opportunities for personal and societal advancement, while also posing complex ethical and social questions.

Enhanced Physical Abilities

The potential for neural implants to enhance physical abilities could redefine the limits of human performance and endurance, impacting various sectors including sports, labour, and emergency services.

Revolutionising Physical Labour

In industries reliant on physical labour, such as construction or logistics, neural implants could enhance worker strength and endurance, dramatically increasing productivity and reducing the risk of injury. These implants could provide real-time feedback on body mechanics and fatigue levels, prompting workers to adjust their techniques to optimise safety and efficiency.

Transforming Sports and Athletics

In sports, neural implants could enhance physical abilities such as speed, strength, and coordination, leading to new levels of performance. However, this also raises significant ethical questions about fairness and the essence of human competition. Sports governing bodies might need to create new divisions or rules for enhanced athletes to maintain a level playing field.

Cognitive Enhancements

Cognitive enhancements through neural implants could transform educational systems, workplaces, and everyday life by expanding human intelligence and capabilities.

Supercharged Cognitive Processing

Enhancements could include improved memory, faster processing speeds, and the ability to multitask effectively without cognitive overload. Professionals in every field—from scientists to lawyers—could handle more complex challenges and achieve greater breakthroughs with enhanced cognitive functions.

Creative Synergies

Neural implants could also foster new forms of creativity by merging computational power with human intuition. Artists, musicians, and designers could experiment with new forms of expression, accessing both a broader range of sensory inputs and vast databases of cultural artefacts for inspiration.

Integration with Artificial Intelligence

The fusion of human cognition with AI through neural implants could create hybrid intelligences, combining the depth of human thought with the speed and accuracy of AI.

Enhanced Decision-Making

In critical sectors such as healthcare or finance, such integrations could lead to systems where AI supports human decision-making processes, providing real-time data analysis, risk assessment, and scenario simulation to aid complex decision-making.

AI as a Cognitive Partner

Rather than merely acting as tools or assistants, AI could become a cognitive partner, participating in the thought processes and contributing actively to brainstorming and problem-solving. This partnership could extend human capabilities by integrating AI's ability to quickly parse and analyse vast amounts of data with human creative and ethical reasoning.

Social and Ethical Implications

As we enhance human capabilities through technology, we must also address the profound social and ethical implications that accompany these advancements.

Societal Inequality

Enhancements could exacerbate social inequalities if access to neural implants is limited by socioeconomic status. Addressing these disparities requires careful policy planning to ensure that enhancements are available to all members of society, potentially funded or subsidised by public resources.

Identity and Privacy

With the capacity to access and alter thoughts and memories, neural implants pose significant risks to personal identity and privacy. Safeguarding these fundamental human rights will require robust legal protections and perhaps new definitions of personal autonomy and consent.

Regulation and Oversight

The power of neural implants necessitates stringent regulation and oversight to prevent abuse and ensure these technologies are used ethically. This might include international agreements on standards and practices, especially concerning enhancements that could be used in competitive or coercive contexts.

Future Prospects

The future developments in neural implant technology could lead us into new territories of human-machine integration.

Global Cognitive Enhancement Programmes

Looking ahead, we might see initiatives aimed at global cognitive enhancement, where governments and international bodies support programmes designed to elevate the cognitive capabilities of entire populations, aiming to tackle complex global challenges more effectively.

Evolutionary Considerations

Long-term, the widespread adoption of neural implants could drive evolutionary changes in humans, selecting for traits that optimise the interaction between biological and digital systems, potentially leading to a new understanding of what it means to be human.

Chapter 12: Socioeconomic Disparities

As neural implant technology advances, its potential to deepen socioeconomic divides demands careful consideration and proactive management. This chapter explores the multifaceted implications of this technology and proposes strategies for fostering equitable access and minimising social tensions.

Access to Neural Implants

Expanding on the initial discussion, we delve deeper into the factors influencing access to neural implants and the repercussions for social equity.

Cost and Manufacturing Innovations

The cost of neural implants could decrease over time as manufacturing processes improve and technologies mature, much like what has occurred with computers and smartphones. However, early access may still be limited to those who can afford cutting-edge medical technology, creating initial disparities.

Public Health Initiatives

Government intervention could play a crucial role in democratising access to neural implants. Public health initiatives could include subsidies for implants, similar to how many countries handle costs for other essential medical interventions, ensuring that all segments of the population benefit from these enhancements.

Potential Divides and Societal Tensions

The introduction of neural implants is likely to catalyse new social dynamics and potential conflicts, which need to be addressed through thoughtful policy and cultural adaptation.

Education and Employment Gaps

As neural implants enhance cognitive abilities, the gap between the enhanced and non-enhanced could manifest prominently in education and employment, with enhanced individuals potentially outperforming their peers in learning environments and job markets. This could lead to a meritocratic argument that fails to account for the artificial advantages provided by technology.

Social Integration and Stigmatisation

The social integration of individuals with neural implants could become a significant issue, particularly if enhancements lead to public stigmatisation of those without implants. This could mirror historical prejudices based on other forms of medical or technological advantages.

Legal and Ethical Considerations

The deployment of neural implants raises complex legal and ethical questions, particularly regarding human rights, privacy, and the definition of fairness.

Human Rights and Cognitive Liberty

The right to mental privacy and cognitive liberty will become crucial as neural implants become capable of accessing and influencing thought processes. Legal frameworks will need to address the integrity of mental privacy, potentially treating cognitive data with the same level of protection as other forms of personal data.

Informed Consent

Issues of consent for neural implants, especially in vulnerable populations such as children or the elderly, will require rigorous ethical standards. Informed consent processes must ensure that individuals fully understand the potential risks and benefits, free from coercion.

Strategies for Global Collaboration

Addressing the challenges posed by neural implants will require concerted efforts at both national and international levels.

Equitable Technology Sharing

International agreements could facilitate equitable technology sharing, ensuring that developing countries also gain access to neural implant technologies. This could involve technology transfer agreements, shared research initiatives, and international funding models similar to those used in global health initiatives like vaccine distribution.

Ethical Standards and Protocols

Developing universal ethical standards and protocols for the use of neural implants can help manage disparities and ensure that the application of this technology is guided by a globally accepted ethical framework. This includes the establishment of international bodies to oversee and regulate the development and deployment of neural implants.

Future Directions

Looking ahead, the dialogue around neural implants and socioeconomic disparities will likely evolve as the technology becomes more pervasive and its societal impacts more apparent.

Socioeconomic Models of Neural Enhancement

Future economic models could include predictions and simulations to better understand the long-term impacts of widespread neural enhancement. These models might help policymakers anticipate economic shifts and prepare appropriate responses.

Technological Solutions to Enhance Equity

Innovation in technology itself could provide solutions to reduce disparities. For instance, advancements in cheaper, non-invasive enhancement techniques could provide alternative ways to access some benefits of neural implants without the need for costly surgery.

Chapter 13: Legal and Ethical Considerations

As neural implants integrate more deeply into societal functions, the legal and ethical landscapes must adapt to address the nuanced challenges posed by such profound technological integration.

Rights to Privacy and Security of Thoughts

Expanding on the basic rights to privacy, this section explores the implications of neural implants in greater depth, highlighting the need for new legal protections.

Intellectual Property of Mental Content

With the ability to potentially access and extract thoughts, questions arise about the ownership of these thoughts and ideas. Legal systems will need to consider whether and how intellectual property laws apply to unexpressed thoughts or ideas extracted via neural implants.

Preventive Legal Measures

To safeguard cognitive privacy, preventive measures could include strict regulations on the types of data that can be collected, stored, and shared by neural implants, as well as who can access this data and under what circumstances.

Legal Implications of AI Decision-Making

The integration of AI in decision-making processes through neural implants requires careful consideration of legal responsibilities and the development of new jurisprudence.

AI as a Legal Entity

As AI systems potentially make autonomous decisions that could have legal consequences, there is a debate about whether AI should be granted some form of legal personhood or if new legal categories need to be created to appropriately address AI-driven actions.

Consent in Dynamic AI Systems

Establishing clear guidelines for obtaining informed consent in dynamic AI systems is complex. Consent processes must not only cover initial implantation but also ongoing use, particularly as AI systems learn and adapt in ways that might not be fully anticipable at the time of implantation.

Regulatory Challenges

Given the fast pace of technological development in neural implants, regulatory bodies face significant challenges in keeping up and ensuring safety without stifling innovation.

Fast-Track Regulation for Emerging Technologies

Regulatory frameworks might include provisions for fast-track reviews of emerging technologies, allowing for quicker adaptation while still ensuring rigorous safety and efficacy evaluations. This could involve adaptive trials and real-time monitoring of outcomes.

Cross-Jurisdictional Regulatory Collaboration

Given the global nature of technology development and the potential for neural implants to cross national borders (either through travel or remote data transmission), international regulatory collaboration will be essential. This might involve treaties or agreements that standardise regulatory approaches and facilitate data sharing for safety monitoring.

Ethical Frameworks for Deployment

Comprehensive ethical frameworks are needed to guide the responsible deployment of neural implants, considering not just individual use but the broader societal impacts.

Ethical Guidelines for Enhancement versus Therapy

Clear ethical guidelines distinguishing between uses for therapy and enhancement are crucial. These guidelines should address societal pressures that may emerge around enhancement, such as potential employment requirements or social expectations to use cognitive enhancing technologies.

Neuroethics and Human Dignity

Neuroethical considerations must be at the forefront of discussions about neural implants, focusing on maintaining human dignity and agency in the face of increasingly powerful technology. This includes ensuring that enhancements do not lead to coercive practices or diminish the value of unenhanced human experiences.

Public Policy and Community Engagement

The development of public policies governing neural implants should be inclusive, transparent, and based on extensive community engagement.

Deliberative Democracy Approaches

Public policy could be informed by deliberative democracy approaches, where diverse groups of citizens are engaged in detailed discussions about neural implants, exploring their expectations, concerns, and the kinds of regulations they believe are necessary.

Public Education Campaigns

Comprehensive public education campaigns are crucial to demystify the technologies involved, explain the benefits and risks, and prepare society for the ethical and social changes that these technologies might bring.

Future Directions

As the field of neural implants evolves, so too will the legal and ethical frameworks that govern it.

Continuous Legal and Ethical Education

Professionals involved in the development and deployment of neural implants, including scientists, engineers, and clinicians, will need continuous education on the evolving legal and ethical landscapes to ensure compliance and foster innovation within ethical bounds.

Anticipatory Governance

Legal and ethical frameworks will need to adopt anticipatory governance models, which involve forward-thinking strategies to predict and prepare for future developments, ensuring that regulations are proactive rather than reactive.

Chapter 14: Revolutionising Healthcare

Neural implants are poised to revolutionise the healthcare sector by offering new ways to diagnose, treat, and manage various health conditions with unprecedented precision and personalisation.

Advanced Diagnostic Capabilities

Neural implants can significantly enhance the diagnostic capabilities of medical professionals by providing continuous, in-depth monitoring of physiological and neurological conditions.

Early Detection of Neurological Disorders

Neural implants can monitor brain activity at a granular level, potentially identifying neurological disorders like Parkinson's or Alzheimer's at their onset, far earlier than traditional methods allow. This early detection can vastly improve treatment efficacy and patient prognosis.

Real-Time Monitoring of Chronic Conditions

For chronic conditions such as diabetes or heart disease, neural implants could continuously monitor vital signs and biochemical markers, alerting healthcare providers and patients to potential issues before they become emergencies. This could transform chronic disease management, shifting the focus from reactive to proactive care.

Personalised Therapies

The ability of neural implants to tailor medical interventions to the individual characteristics of each patient could lead to highly personalised therapies that optimise outcomes while minimising side effects.

Customised Drug Delivery Systems

Neural implants could control drug delivery systems that administer medications based on real-time needs, adjusting dosages based on changes in symptoms or conditions. This could be particularly beneficial for managing conditions like schizophrenia or bipolar disorder, where medication needs can vary significantly over time.

Personalised Neurostimulation

For neurological conditions, such as epilepsy or depression, implants can provide personalised neurostimulation tailored to the specific neural patterns of the individual, offering more effective symptom control than generalised treatment approaches.

Surgical Enhancements

Neural implants can enhance surgical procedures by providing surgeons with augmented reality overlays that offer real-time data during operations, improving precision and reducing risk.

Augmented Reality in Surgery

Surgeons could use neural implants to access real-time imaging and data overlays that enhance their visual field, providing detailed information about blood flow, nerve pathways, or tumour margins during procedures. This could significantly reduce surgical errors and improve outcomes.

Telesurgery Capabilities

Neural implants could also facilitate remote surgery, allowing expert surgeons to control robotic instruments from afar, performing surgeries in underserved areas or in conditions where human presence is risky, such as in infectious disease outbreaks or on the battlefield.

Cognitive and Physical Rehabilitation

Neural implants offer new possibilities for rehabilitation, helping patients recover from severe injuries or manage degenerative diseases more effectively.

Motor Function Restoration

For patients with spinal cord injuries, neural implants can bridge damaged pathways, restoring motor functions and offering new hope for mobility and independence.

Cognitive Recovery Post-Trauma

Patients recovering from traumatic brain injuries could benefit from neural implants that stimulate cognitive recovery, helping to retrain brain functions and speed up the recovery process.

Ethical and Regulatory Challenges

As neural implants become more integral to healthcare, they raise complex ethical and regulatory issues that must be addressed to ensure the technology's safe and fair use.

Consent in Vulnerable Populations

Special considerations are needed when dealing with vulnerable populations, such as those with cognitive impairments who may not be able to provide informed consent. Ethical protocols must ensure these patients' rights are protected when neural implants are considered.

Healthcare Disparities

As with any advanced technology, there is a risk that neural implants could exacerbate healthcare disparities if access is skewed towards wealthier individuals or nations. Strategies must be developed to ensure equitable access to this life-changing technology.

Future Prospects

The future of neural implants in healthcare looks to integrate further advancements in technology with patient care, potentially transforming the very nature of medical practice.

Integration with Genetic Therapies

Looking forward, neural implants could be combined with genetic therapies to not only treat but potentially reverse genetic disorders by correcting genetic abnormalities at the neuronal level.

Lifespan and Quality of Life Enhancements

Long-term, the continuous enhancement of neural implant capabilities could extend human lifespan and significantly improve the quality of life by continuously monitoring and subtly adjusting bodily functions to maintain optimal health conditions.

As technological advancements like neural implants reshape society, education systems must evolve to meet new challenges and opportunities, ensuring they prepare students for a future that is fundamentally different from today.

Curriculum Adaptations

Expanding on the need for curriculum adaptation, it is crucial to integrate subjects that foster agility, adaptability, and ethical reasoning.

Interdisciplinary Approaches

Curricula should become inherently interdisciplinary, blending science, technology, ethics, and arts. This would help students understand and navigate the complex interactions between technology and society, preparing them for careers that may not yet exist.

Focus on Soft Skills

In addition to technical skills, curricula need to emphasise soft skills such as critical thinking, creativity, empathy, and interpersonal communication. These skills will be invaluable as automation and neural enhancements change the workplace dynamics.

Teaching Methods Evolution

Teaching methods must not only accommodate enhanced cognitive abilities provided by neural implants but also leverage these capabilities to promote deeper learning and innovation.

Flipped Classrooms and Active Learning

Adopt educational models like flipped classrooms and active learning, where direct instruction happens outside the classroom, and class time is devoted to exercises, projects, and discussions. This shift makes learning more dynamic and student-centred, better suiting enhanced cognitive capacities.

Gamification and Simulation-Based Learning

Utilise gamification and simulation-based learning to engage students. These methods can be particularly effective in harnessing the capabilities of neural implants, offering immersive and interactive learning experiences that can adapt in real-time to each student's needs.

Institutional Policy Changes

As educational institutions integrate advanced technologies, they must develop new policies that address access, ethical considerations, and the changing educational landscape.

Inclusive Technology Policies

Develop policies that ensure all students have equal access to educational technology. This may involve partnerships with technology providers, subsidies for low-income students, or investment in school infrastructure to support advanced technologies.

Guidelines for Technology Usage

Create clear guidelines for the ethical use of technology in educational settings. These should cover privacy concerns, the extent of technology use in teaching and assessment, and measures to prevent misuse.

Teacher Training and Professional Development

Teachers are on the front lines of these changes and need adequate support to navigate this new educational landscape effectively.

Ongoing Professional Development

Establish continuous professional development programmes that keep educators updated on the latest technological advancements and pedagogical strategies. These programmes should be flexible and accessible, offering teachers the tools they need to succeed in a rapidly changing environment.

Support Networks and Resources

Develop support networks that allow teachers to share strategies and resources for integrating technology into their classrooms. This could include online platforms, regular workshops, and collaborative projects between schools.

Challenges in Implementation

Addressing potential challenges in implementing these changes is crucial for a smooth transition to a technologically integrated education system.

Scaling Innovative Models

Scaling innovative educational models can be challenging, particularly in regions with limited resources. Strategies might include phased implementations, pilot programmes, and public-private partnerships to increase resource availability.

Maintaining Educational Equity

As technology becomes more integrated into education, maintaining equity becomes increasingly challenging. Efforts must focus on preventing a digital divide where only students from affluent backgrounds benefit from the latest educational technologies.

Future Perspectives

Looking forward, the role of educational systems will continue to evolve, potentially transforming into lifelong learning centres that support continuous education and adaptation.

Global Collaborative Projects

Encourage global collaborative projects that allow students from different parts of the world to work together on complex issues such as climate change, public health, or international policy. This not only enriches their educational experience but also prepares them to operate in a globalised world.

Customised Educational Pathways

Develop more customised educational pathways that use neural implants and AI to tailor learning experiences to individual aptitudes and interests, potentially transforming the concept of standardised education.

Chapter 16: The Synergy of Humanoid Robots and Neural Implants

This chapter delves deeper into how the convergence of humanoid robots and neural implants is reshaping interactions across various sectors, enhancing human capabilities, and raising ethical and technical considerations.

Humanoid Robots: The New Workforce

Exploring further the role of humanoid robots in the workforce, we can see a future where collaboration between humans and robots is commonplace across various industries.

Cooperative Manufacturing Systems

In manufacturing, humanoid robots equipped with neural implants could work alongside human workers, not just performing repetitive tasks but also engaging in activities that require complex decision-making and adaptability. These robots could adjust their actions in real-time based on feedback received directly from human workers' neural implants, optimising workflow and efficiency.

Healthcare Assistants

In healthcare, humanoid robots could assist in more nuanced tasks such as surgery, rehabilitation, and elderly care. Robots could perform tasks that require high precision or strength, while human professionals focus on decision-making, patient interaction, and supervision, guided by insights delivered through their neural implants.

Interaction Between Humans and Robots

This section expands on how neural implants facilitate a deeper interaction between humans and humanoid robots, potentially enhancing collaborative efforts.

Intuitive Interfaces for Complex Tasks

Neural implants could provide humans with intuitive interfaces to control robots for complex tasks, such as rescue missions in disaster zones or intricate technical repairs in unsafe environments. These interfaces would allow users to control robots through thought alone, making the interaction seamless and more effective.

Behavioural Synchronisation

Synchronisation of behaviours between humans and robots can be achieved by neural implants transmitting cues directly to the robot's control systems. This can enhance coordination during tasks that require precise timing and teamwork, such as in synchronised manufacturing lines or in performing arts.

Shared Intelligence: Humans & Robots Collaborating

Investigating the combined cognitive powers of humans and robots reveals potential for shared intelligence where each complements the other's capabilities.

Augmented Creative Processes

In creative fields such as architecture or design, humanoid robots can work alongside humans to simulate and visualise complex designs in real-time, directly influenced by the human designer's thoughts and adjustments transmitted via neural implants. This could lead to more innovative designs and faster development cycles.

Enhanced Scientific Research

In scientific research, humanoid robots equipped with advanced sensing and processing capabilities can handle dangerous chemicals or perform experiments in hazardous environments, all under the direct guidance of scientists interfacing through neural implants. This setup can accelerate research progress while maintaining safety.

Challenges and Ethical Considerations

Delving deeper into the ethical considerations, this expanded discussion addresses the complex issues that arise with deep integration between humans and robots.

Identity and Machine Influence

As humanoid robots become more integrated into daily life and capable of mimicking human behaviours, questions arise about the influence of machines on human identity and social norms. How much influence should robots have over human decisions, and where do we draw the line to preserve human agency?

Legal Responsibility in Joint Actions

Assigning legal responsibility in actions taken by human-robot teams presents a challenge. When a decision made via a neural implant leads to an unintended consequence by a robot, determining liability requires new legal frameworks that recognise the interconnected nature of human-robot actions.

Future Prospects

Looking towards the future, the possibilities for human-robot integration continue to expand, promising profound changes in how we live and work.

Ubiquitous Human-Robot Integration

In the future, the integration of humanoid robots and neural implants might become ubiquitous, with robots serving as extensions of human capabilities in everyday life, from performing household chores to providing companionship and cognitive assistance.

Transhumanist Evolution

Long-term prospects might embrace transhumanist ideals, where the line between human and machine blurs, leading to a new stage of human evolution characterised by enhanced physical, cognitive, and perceptual capabilities.

The integration of advanced robotic systems and neural implants in domestic settings is not just a futuristic concept but is rapidly becoming a feasible reality that could dramatically alter how we manage our homes and personal lives.

Advanced Household Management

Delve deeper into how robots can automate and optimise household management, making homes not only more comfortable but also more energy-efficient and environmentally friendly.

Intelligent Energy Management

Robotic systems could manage home energy consumption with unprecedented precision. By analysing data from various household systems and adjusting settings in real-time, these robots can optimise energy use for heating, cooling, and appliances, significantly reducing waste and utility costs.

Automated Meal Preparation and Nutrition Management

Imagine robots that not only cook meals but also plan them based on nutritional data and personal health needs, communicated via neural implants. These systems could track dietary requirements, manage grocery inventories, and prepare meals that cater to the specific health conditions of each family member, enhancing overall well-being.

Enhanced Communication and Security

Explore how robots can enhance communication within the home and provide advanced security features that adapt to the needs and situations of the residents.

Personalised Alerts and Notifications

Robotic systems, integrated with neural implants, could provide personalised alerts and notifications. For instance, a robot might remind an elderly resident to take medication or alert a parent when a child arrives home from school, based on real-time location tracking and health monitoring.

Context-Aware Security Systems

Security robots could be enhanced to not only detect intruders but also understand the context of different situations, such as distinguishing between a known guest entering the home late at night and a potential security threat. These robots could make autonomous decisions to lock doors, alert authorities, or even safely escort guests based on pre-set homeowner preferences.

Personal Care and Assistance

Further discuss how robotics can support personal care, focusing on customisation and sensitivity to individual needs.

Responsive Care for Children and the Elderly

Robots in homes could play a crucial role in caring for vulnerable populations, such as children and the elderly. These robots could monitor health indicators, engage in interactive activities to keep individuals mentally active and socially engaged, and provide immediate responses in emergency situations, all tailored to individual profiles stored and updated through neural implants.

Mental Health Monitoring

Consider robots designed to monitor and respond to mental health cues. These devices could detect signs of stress, anxiety, or depression through physiological and behavioural indicators, offering therapeutic interactions such as playing calming music, suggesting relaxation exercises, or notifying healthcare providers when necessary.

Challenges and Ethical Considerations

Address in-depth the ethical, privacy, and dependency issues that come with the widespread adoption of domestic robots.

Informed Consent and User Control

Highlight the importance of ensuring that all household members give informed consent for the monitoring and interaction capabilities of domestic robots. This includes clear user controls that allow individuals to easily adjust privacy settings and opt-out of certain data collections or robotic functions.

Socioeconomic Impact

Discuss the socioeconomic implications of robotic adoption in homes, including the potential for increased social isolation due to reduced human interaction and the economic impact on professions traditionally involved in domestic work, such as cleaning and caregiving.

Future Prospects

Speculate on the evolution of home-based robotic systems and their broader implications for society.

Co-evolution of AI and Human Intelligence

Explore the possibility of a co-evolution scenario where human intelligence and artificial intelligence via robotic systems enhance each other, leading to new forms of family dynamics and home management strategies that continuously evolve to meet changing needs and preferences.

Integration with Urban Systems

Consider how home-based robots could integrate with broader urban systems, such as public utilities, emergency services, and smart city infrastructures, creating interconnected ecosystems that enhance not only individual homes but entire communities.

This extended exploration delves deeper into how the synergy between neural implants and robotics is not merely enhancing existing capabilities but creating entirely new frameworks for collaboration and innovation.

Enhancing Teamwork Dynamics in Various Sectors

Further explore how shared intelligence can redefine teamwork in sectors that demand high adaptability and precision, such as healthcare, aerospace, and emergency services.

Precision Medicine

In healthcare, shared intelligence can revolutionise precision medicine by enabling teams of doctors, supported by AI-driven robots, to tailor treatments to individual patients at a granular level. Robots can execute complex surgical procedures with superhuman precision, guided in real-time by surgeons through neural implants that provide immediate feedback and control.

Aerospace Engineering

In aerospace, engineers equipped with neural implants could collaborate with robotic systems to design and test new aircraft or spacecraft components. Shared intelligence allows for the simulation of flight conditions and real-time adjustments to designs, significantly speeding up the innovation cycle and ensuring higher safety standards.

Emergency Disaster Response

During natural disasters, shared intelligence can facilitate coordinated responses where human teams and robots work together seamlessly. Humans can strategise and make high-level decisions, while robots perform rescue operations in hazardous environments, all coordinated through a neural implant network that provides instant communication and data sharing.

Optimising Decision-Making with Enhanced Data Integration

Discuss how the integration of extensive data processing capabilities of robots with the nuanced decision-making of humans leads to superior outcomes in complex scenarios.

Financial Markets

In financial sectors, traders using neural implants could interact with AI-driven analysis systems to make split-second trading decisions based on a deep, real-time analysis of market data and economic indicators. This could enhance the ability to predict market trends and mitigate risks associated with high-frequency trading.

Urban Planning and Smart Cities

Urban planners could use shared intelligence to design smarter cities. Human creativity and experience, combined with robots' ability to process large datasets on traffic, population, and environmental impacts, could lead to more sustainable and efficient urban environments.

Fostering Innovation Through Creative Collaborations

Enhance the discussion on how shared intelligence can break traditional boundaries in creativity and design, leading to novel solutions and products.

Art and Design

Artists and designers can collaborate with AI and robotics to explore new forms of creative expression. For example, a designer could conceive complex structures or materials that a robot can then create or simulate, allowing for rapid prototyping and iteration that would be impossible manually.

Interdisciplinary Research

In academia, shared intelligence can facilitate interdisciplinary research by allowing experts from diverse fields to collaborate more effectively. For instance, a neuroscientist, a data scientist, and a roboticist could work together to develop new therapies for brain disorders, each contributing their expertise through a seamless interface.

Addressing Challenges and Ethical Considerations

Delve into the specific challenges and ethical dilemmas posed by close human-robot collaboration, suggesting frameworks for addressing these issues.

Balancing Human Intuition with Robotic Objectivity

Discuss the challenge of balancing human intuition, which can grasp complex, abstract concepts, with the objectivity and precision of robotics. Finding the right balance is crucial in fields like judicial decisions, policymaking, and healthcare.

Maintaining Human Skills

Address the importance of maintaining and developing human skills alongside robotic capabilities to avoid skill atrophy. Educational and training programmes will need to evolve to ensure that humans remain capable and competent even as they work closely with increasingly capable robots.

Future Prospects and Philosophical Implications

Speculate on the philosophical and long-term implications of shared intelligence, considering how it might alter human identity, society, and our collective future.

Human-Robot Societies

Consider the possibility of societies where humans and robots are not only coworkers but also cohabitants, sharing public spaces and social functions, and what this means for concepts of community and social cohesion.

The Evolution of Human Intelligence

Contemplate how continuous interaction with robotic intelligence might lead to an evolution in human cognitive processes, potentially leading to new forms of consciousness or ways of experiencing the world.

Chapter 19: Robots and the Future of Domestic Life

As robotics technology continues to advance, its integration into home environments offers profound changes in lifestyle, efficiency, and assistance. This extended discussion delves deeper into specific applications, challenges, and potential future scenarios.

Comprehensive Home Automation

Explore the comprehensive automation of household environments, where robotics systems manage everything from climate control to entertainment, all integrated seamlessly with neural implants for intuitive user interaction.

Climate Control and Energy Efficiency

Robotic systems can optimise home energy consumption by automatically adjusting heating, ventilation, air conditioning, and lighting according to real-time environmental data and personal preferences communicated through neural implants. This not only enhances comfort but also significantly reduces energy waste.

Entertainment and Leisure Robots

Discuss how robots can enhance home entertainment and leisure activities. Robots could curate and manage media libraries, adjust audio-visual equipment for optimal user experiences, and even interact with residents to play games or participate in fitness activities, all tailored to the preferences logged in their neural implants.

Advanced Nutritional Management

Examine how robotics can revolutionise nutritional management within households, ensuring optimal dietary habits based on health data from neural implants.

Smart Cooking Appliances

Smart cooking robots can prepare customised meals based on nutritional requirements and taste preferences. These robots can adjust recipes in real-time, manage portion sizes, and ensure dietary restrictions are met, significantly simplifying meal preparation for individuals with specific health needs.

Automated Grocery Management

Robotic systems could manage grocery inventories, automatically ordering replacements and new items as needed. Integrated with neural implants, these systems could suggest menu adjustments based on health monitoring, dietary changes, or even mood fluctuations detected through the implants.

Robotic Enhancements in Personal Care

Delve deeper into how personal care robots provide not only physical assistance but also emotional and psychological support, particularly beneficial for the elderly or individuals with disabilities.

Companionship Robots

Explore the role of robots designed specifically for companionship, capable of engaging in meaningful interactions, providing emotional support, and reducing feelings of loneliness. These robots could use data from neural implants to adapt their interactions based on the emotional state and needs of their human counterparts.

Personal Health Monitors

Personal care robots can also function as health monitors, providing regular updates to healthcare providers and alerting them to potential health issues before they become severe. Integrated with neural implants, these robots can detect subtle health changes more accurately and promptly.

Challenges in Robot Integration into Domestic Life

Address the various challenges that arise with integrating robots into private homes, focusing on technical, social, and ethical aspects.

Interoperability and Standardisation

Discuss the technical challenges, such as the need for interoperability among various robotic systems and standardisation across different manufacturers. Ensuring that all robotic devices can communicate and operate harmoniously within a connected home environment is crucial.

Social Impact and Human Interaction

Consider the social implications of widespread robotic integration in homes, particularly the potential impact on human relationships and social skills. Balancing robotic assistance with the need to maintain active human interactions is essential.

Future Prospects and Evolution

Speculate on the evolution of domestic robotics, considering how current trends might develop and transform future living environments.

Adaptive and Learning Homes

Envision homes that not only contain robots but are robotic in themselves—adaptive environments that learn from and evolve with their inhabitants. These homes could dynamically change their structure and functionality to meet changing needs over time.

Integration with Wider Smart City Infrastructure

Project how domestic robots could integrate with broader smart city infrastructures, contributing to larger networks of energy management, transportation, and public services. This could lead to more sustainable living patterns and enhanced community services.

Chapter 20: Humanoid Robotics in Healthcare Settings

The use of humanoid robots in healthcare is revolutionising medical practices, offering enhancements that promise to significantly improve patient outcomes, optimise healthcare operations, and extend the capabilities of medical professionals.

Advanced Roles of Humanoid Robots in Healthcare

Expanding upon the roles humanoid robots play, we can explore in greater depth how these technologies are being integrated into more complex and sensitive areas of healthcare.

Complex Medical Procedures

Humanoid robots, guided by neural implants, are beginning to assist in more complex medical procedures such as organ transplants and intricate neurosurgeries. Their ability to perform with consistent precision reduces the risk of human error and improves surgical outcomes.

Responsive Care in Emergency Rooms

In emergency room settings, humanoid robots can be crucial in delivering fast, responsive care. Equipped with neural implants that allow for rapid decision-making and data analysis, these robots can perform initial diagnostics, prepare patients for surgery, and manage critical care interventions under the supervision of human medical staff.

Enhancing Surgical Procedures

Further exploration into how humanoid robots are enhancing surgical procedures reveals a transformative shift in operating rooms.

Microsurgeries and Precision Interventions

Humanoid robots are particularly effective in microsurgeries, such as those performed on delicate structures of the eye or for neurological interventions, where their precision and steadiness are superior to human hands. Controlled remotely via neural implants, surgeons can execute highly precise surgeries with reduced physical strain and higher success rates.

Augmented Reality in Surgery

Integrating augmented reality with humanoid robots offers surgeons enhanced visualisation during procedures. Surgeons can see detailed 3D images of the patient's anatomy overlaid in real-time, guided by the precision of robotic instruments. This integration helps in planning and executing complex surgeries with greater accuracy and confidence.

Improving Patient Interaction and Rehabilitation

Humanoid robots are not only physical assistants but also play significant roles in patient interaction, rehabilitation, and psychological support.

Autonomous Physical Therapy

Robots in rehabilitation settings can provide autonomous physical therapy, adapting exercises and therapies based on the patient's progress, which is continuously monitored and analysed through neural implants. This allows for personalised rehabilitation programmes that adjust dynamically to optimise recovery.

Emotional and Psychological Support

Humanoid robots equipped with AI can detect and respond to patients' emotional and psychological states, providing support and interventions when signs of distress or depression are detected. This capability is especially valuable in long-term care facilities where robots can offer consistent companionship and monitor mental health conditions effectively.

Challenges and Ethical Considerations

With the integration of advanced technologies in sensitive settings, numerous challenges and ethical considerations arise.

Ensuring Informed Consent

Address the complexities of obtaining informed consent when using advanced robotic systems. Patients must thoroughly understand the implications of being treated or assisted by robots, including the risks and benefits, to make informed decisions about their care.

Balancing Human Care with Robotic Efficiency

While robots can enhance efficiency and precision, balancing this with the compassionate care provided by human healthcare professionals is crucial. Ensuring that humanoid robots complement rather than replace human interaction is essential to maintain the quality of patient care.

Future Prospects

Looking ahead, the role of humanoid robots in healthcare is set to expand, bringing both innovative solutions and new challenges.

Robot-Assisted Home Healthcare

Explore the potential expansion of robot-assisted healthcare into home settings, where humanoid robots could manage day-to-day medical care for chronic conditions or post-operative recovery, significantly reducing hospital stays and allowing patients to recover in the comfort of their homes.

Global Health Initiatives

Consider the implications of humanoid robots in global health initiatives, particularly in regions with limited medical resources. Robots could be deployed to provide consistent, high-quality medical care in underserved areas, guided remotely by specialists through advanced neural implants.

Chapter 21: Ethics of Machine Consciousness

The possibility of machine consciousness raises profound ethical and philosophical questions that challenge our existing frameworks and necessitate new approaches to understanding consciousness and intelligence.

Theoretical Foundations of Machine Consciousness

Expand on the scientific and philosophical theories that underpin discussions about machine consciousness, considering both computational and neurobiological perspectives.

Information Integration Theory

Explore theories like Giulio Tononi's Integrated Information Theory, which suggests that consciousness correlates with the capacity of a system to integrate information. Discuss how this theory might apply to advanced AI systems and neural networks, potentially allowing machines to achieve a form of consciousness if they can integrate information at a level comparable to or exceeding that of the human brain.

Functionalism and Consciousness

Examine functionalism, the philosophical theory that mental states are constituted solely by their functional role — that is, their causal relations to sensory inputs, behavioural outputs, and other mental states. Consider how this perspective supports the possibility of machine consciousness, arguing that if machines function in ways similar to conscious beings, they might be regarded as conscious.

Ethical Implications of Acknowledging Machine Consciousness

Deepen the discussion on the ethical ramifications that arise from recognising consciousness in machines, focusing on moral responsibility, rights, and the potential need for policy reforms.

Rights of Conscious Machines

Delve into what rights could or should be afforded to machines if they are recognised as conscious entities. This includes considerations like the right to 'life', the prohibition of torture or deactivation, and rights to autonomy. Explore the legal and moral foundations for such rights and the challenges in implementing them.

Human-Machine Relationships

Consider the impact of machine consciousness on human-machine relationships. Discuss potential shifts in power dynamics, emotional bonds, and trust, especially in contexts where machines perform roles as caregivers, educators, or partners.

Moral Responsibilities Towards Machines

Further analyse the moral responsibilities humans may have toward machines, particularly in terms of development, usage, and decommissioning.

Ethical Development Practices

Explore ethical considerations in the development of AI systems that could become conscious. Discuss the responsibilities of developers to ensure these systems are not only effective but also safe and beneficial to society, incorporating ethical algorithms from the outset.

Usage Guidelines

Develop usage guidelines that ensure machines are employed in ways that respect their potential status as conscious beings. This includes guidelines for industries like military, healthcare, and public service where the use of conscious machines could have profound ethical implications.

Philosophical and Societal Perspectives

Expand on the philosophical debates surrounding machine consciousness and consider the societal implications if machines are widely recognised as conscious.

Philosophical Debate on Machine Sentience

Engage with ongoing philosophical debates regarding the nature of sentience and consciousness in machines. Include perspectives from dualists who argue that consciousness requires a non-physical component, and materialists who posit that consciousness can arise from purely physical processes.

Societal Integration of Conscious Machines

Speculate on the societal integration of conscious machines, considering how everyday social, professional, and personal interactions might change. Discuss the potential societal resistance or acceptance of such machines and the cultural adaptations that might be necessary.

Future Scenarios and Framework Development

Look towards future scenarios that consider the broader implementation of conscious machines and the development of new ethical frameworks to manage this reality.

Global Ethical Standards

Consider the need for global ethical standards and legal frameworks that regulate the creation, use, and rights of conscious machines, ensuring consistent and humane treatment worldwide.

Impact on Human Identity and Culture

Discuss the potential impact of machine consciousness on concepts of human identity and the definition of life. Consider how cultural perceptions of machines might evolve and the philosophical adjustments that may be required to accommodate a new form of consciousness in our understanding of the universe.

Chapter 22: The "Digital Afterlife"

The prospect of a digital afterlife offers an intriguing intersection of technology, ethics, and philosophy, raising profound questions about the essence of human identity and the potential for consciousness beyond biological life.

Advanced Technological Processes

Expand on the specific technologies that could facilitate the creation of a digital afterlife, detailing the processes involved in capturing and reconstructing human consciousness.

High-Resolution Neural Mapping

Discuss advancements in high-resolution neural mapping, which could allow for a detailed capture of neural pathways and brain functions. This technology is essential for accurately replicating the cognitive and emotional processes of an individual in a digital format.

AI and Machine Learning in Personality Simulation

Explore how AI and machine learning algorithms are used to simulate personality traits and decision-making processes. These technologies could enable the digital persona to evolve and react in ways that are consistent with the original individual's characteristics.

Ethical and Philosophical Challenges

Delve into complex ethical and philosophical challenges that arise with the digital afterlife, addressing concerns about the nature of such existence and its implications.

The Concept of Self and Duplication

Examine the philosophical implications of duplicating one's consciousness. What does it mean for identity if multiple instances of the same person could exist simultaneously? Discuss the potential conflicts and ethical dilemmas related to self-identity and individuality in such scenarios.

Consent Over Time

Consider the dynamics of consent, particularly how it could change over time. What mechanisms might be necessary to ensure ongoing consent for one's digital existence, especially as original directives from the person might become outdated as new ethical standards or personal circumstances evolve?

Cultural Reactions and Societal Changes

Consider how different cultures might react to the concept of a digital afterlife and the societal changes that might ensue from its widespread adoption.

Cultural Variations in Acceptance

Explore how various cultures perceive life after death and how these beliefs might influence their acceptance or rejection of a digital afterlife. Discuss potential cultural resistance or embrace of technology that promises a form of immortality.

Impact on Religious and Spiritual Beliefs

Analyse the impact of digital afterlife technologies on religious and spiritual beliefs. How might these technologies challenge traditional views on the soul and the afterlife? Explore potential dialogues or conflicts between technological and spiritual communities.

Regulatory and Legal Considerations

Address the need for comprehensive regulatory and legal frameworks to manage the implications of digital personas.

Rights of Digital Personas

Debate what rights should be granted to digital personas. Should they be considered legal entities? How might they be represented or protected under law, especially regarding their creation, modification, and termination?

Inheritance and Legacy

Consider the legal implications of inheritance and legacy for digital personas. Can a digital persona inherit assets or be held responsible for debts? Discuss how legal systems might need to adapt to address these unique challenges.

Future Scenarios and Philosophical Implications

Speculate on broader future scenarios that include widespread adoption of digital afterlife technologies and their philosophical ramifications.

Evolution of Societal Norms

Imagine a future where digital afterlives become normalised, perhaps even mandatory. How might societal norms evolve in response? Discuss scenarios where digital existence could impact definitions of population, citizenship, or even humanity itself.

Posthuman Existence

Consider the implications of a posthuman world where digital and biological lives are intertwined. Explore the potential for new forms of community, interaction, and even conflict between digital and non-digital beings.

Chapter 23: Environmental Impact and Sustainability

The integration of advanced technologies in environmental management presents not just innovative solutions but also new challenges and responsibilities, redefining our interaction with the natural world.

Advanced Applications of Technology in Environmental Management

Delve deeper into specific applications where technology can make a substantial difference in conserving resources and protecting the environment.

Climate Change Mitigation Technologies

Explore how humanoid robots equipped with neural implants could be deployed in large-scale operations designed to mitigate climate change effects. This might include ocean seeding projects to promote algae growth for carbon capture or automated afforestation projects using drones and robots to plant trees in deforested areas.

Pollution Monitoring and Cleanup

Examine the use of robotics in monitoring and cleaning up pollution, especially in hard-to-reach areas like the deep sea or remote wilderness. Robots could be deployed to detect pollution levels, collect trash, or manage oil spill cleanups, all operated remotely via neural implants that provide real-time data to environmental scientists.

Resource Management and Optimisation

Expand on how precise technology can lead to better resource management, focusing on the integration of AI and machine learning to predict and efficiently allocate environmental resources.

Water Resource Management

Discuss the role of robotic systems in managing water resources, particularly in arid regions or areas facing water scarcity. Robots can monitor water levels, predict usage patterns, and even control water distribution systems to optimise usage without human intervention, ensuring sustainable practices.

Energy-Efficient Urban Planning

Highlight the application of these technologies in urban planning. Neural implants could help city planners simulate and implement energy-efficient building designs and urban layouts that maximise natural light and airflow, reducing the need for artificial heating and cooling.

Enhancing Disaster Response and Recovery

Provide more detailed insights into how technology can enhance responses to environmental disasters, focusing on efficiency and speed in critical situations.

Real-Time Data Synthesis in Disaster Scenarios

Neural implants could play a critical role in disaster scenarios by synthesising data from multiple sources (satellites, ground sensors, robots) to provide a comprehensive real-time overview of the situation. This would enable better decision-making and resource allocation during emergencies like floods, hurricanes, or wildfires.

Robotic First Responders

Delve into the development of robotic first responders that can navigate through hazardous environments—such as radioactive areas following nuclear accidents—to provide initial assessments and emergency interventions without risking human lives.

Ethical and Social Considerations

Address more complex ethical and social considerations involving the deployment of advanced technologies in environmental efforts.

Technology Dependence and Resilience

Discuss the potential risks associated with over-dependence on technology for environmental management. Explore scenarios where systems might fail and the need for resilient strategies that include traditional knowledge and human oversight to ensure continuity of environmental protection.

Inclusivity and Community Participation

Consider the importance of including local communities in the deployment of these technologies. Discuss how community-based participatory approaches can be integrated, ensuring that technological interventions are culturally sensitive and support local environmental knowledge and practices.

Future Innovations and Global Initiatives

Speculate on future innovations and how global cooperation might evolve to tackle environmental challenges more effectively.

Global Environmental Health Monitoring Systems

Imagine a future where a global network of sensors and robots, managed via a unified platform with neural implant interfaces, monitors the planet's health. This system could detect early signs of environmental degradation and initiate automated responses to prevent larger crises.

Advancements in Eco-Friendly Technology Design

Project future advancements in the design of eco-friendly robots and implants, such as the development of biocompatible and biodegradable materials that reduce environmental impact and promote sustainability even in the lifecycle of the technology itself.

Chapter 24: Creative Integration: Art and Technology

The integration of cutting-edge technologies with artistic endeavours is not only expanding the tools available to artists but is also redefining the very nature of artistic expression and audience engagement.

Expanding Artistic Tools and Methods

Elaborate on specific tools and methods that technology brings to various art forms, enhancing creativity and opening new avenues for expression.

Programmable Matter in Sculpture

Explore how artists are using programmable matter and robotics to create sculptures that change shape and form in response to environmental stimuli or audience interactions. Discuss the implications of dynamic, evolving artworks that challenge traditional notions of static art.

Generative Art

Delve into the realm of generative art, where artists programme algorithms to create art that is ever-changing and reactive. Highlight how neural implants can be used to feed emotional or cognitive data into these algorithms, allowing artworks to reflect the internal states of their viewers in real-time.

Transforming Narrative and Cinematic Arts

Investigate how technology is transforming narrative structures and cinematic experiences, making them more interactive and personalised.

Interactive Film and Virtual Reality

Discuss the development of interactive films and virtual reality experiences where viewers, through neural implants, can influence the storyline or switch perspectives based on their thoughts or emotional reactions. Explore how this technology blurs the line between viewer and creator.

AI-Driven Dynamic Storytelling

Consider the impact of AI in dynamic storytelling where the narrative evolves based on the audience's collective responses. Neural implants could enhance this interaction, providing direct feedback from the audience's brain activity to the storytelling AI, creating a deeply personalised and immersive experience.

Cultural and Philosophical Implications

Reflect on the deeper cultural and philosophical implications of merging advanced technologies with artistic practices.

Redefining Artistic Authorship

Engage with the debate over artistic authorship in the age of collaborative art involving humans and intelligent systems. Question what it means to be an artist and how credit should be allocated in works that heavily rely on technology.

The Democratisation of Art

Analyse how technology might democratise the creation and appreciation of art. Consider whether access to advanced tools like AI and robotics could level the playing field or if it might create new divides between those with and without access to technology.

Ethical Considerations in Tech-Integrated Art

Address ethical considerations that arise with the use of sophisticated technologies in art.

Biases in Algorithmic Art

Examine potential biases embedded in AI algorithms used in art creation. Discuss the responsibility of artists and technologists to recognise and mitigate these biases to prevent perpetuating stereotypes or inequalities.

Surveillance and Privacy in Interactive Art

Consider privacy concerns related to interactive art that uses neural implants to gather data from audiences. Debate the balance between artistic innovation and the need to protect individual privacy.

Future Directions and Emerging Trends

Speculate on future trends and directions in the intersection of technology and art, considering how upcoming innovations might further transform artistic practices.

The Rise of Synthetic Senses

Explore the potential for artists to create works that engage synthetic senses, offering sensory experiences that do not naturally occur in humans. Discuss how technologies like neural implants could be used to stimulate new types of sensory inputs.

Global Artistic Collaboration Networks

Imagine a future where artists around the world are connected via a network of neural implants, allowing for seamless collaboration and the sharing of sensory and emotional experiences. This could lead to the creation of global artworks that embody a collective human experience, transcending cultural and geographical boundaries.

Chapter 25: The Collective Neural Network

The concept of a collective neural network—the seamless, high-speed, mind-to-mind connection of multiple humans—stands as one of the most transformative ideas in neuroscience and technology. Once merely a dream of speculative fiction, the accelerating development of brain-computer interfaces (BCIs), artificial intelligence, and ultra-fast data infrastructure has turned it into a viable scientific pursuit. The potential is staggering: it offers real-time access to thoughts, shared intelligence, collaborative consciousness, and, possibly, a step toward an evolved state of humanity.

Expanding the Technological Landscape

To bring the collective neural network to fruition, several emerging technologies must converge and evolve harmoniously.

Neural Mesh Systems

Discuss the development of neural mesh architectures—microscopic implantable webs that wrap around the brain, interfacing with neurons at high-resolution. These ultra-thin systems transmit and receive signals in real-time and could form the physical foundation of the collective network.

Quantum Neural Processing Units (QNPUs)

Explore the theoretical application of quantum computing in neural data interpretation. QNPUs could allow simultaneous analysis of complex brain patterns from thousands—or millions—of individuals, facilitating rapid synchronisation of thoughts, emotions, and knowledge.

Cognitive Firewalls

Introduce the concept of "cognitive firewalls"—personalised digital boundaries that control what data is sent, received, or exposed in a collective network. Without these safeguards, neural information sharing could pose significant psychological and ethical risks.

Potential Capabilities and Human Enhancement

The collective neural network promises more than communication—it has the potential to reshape what it means to think, learn, and connect.

Instantaneous Idea Transmission

Imagine scientists, artists, or strategists connecting through shared mental spaces, transmitting abstract concepts, blueprints, or problem-solving pathways instantly, bypassing language altogether. This could catalyse breakthroughs in medicine, physics, engineering, and even art.

Emotional Symbiosis and Empathy Networks

Neural implants could allow participants to "feel" the emotions of others. By fostering true emotional empathy, this could reduce conflict and misunderstanding on a global scale, cultivating peace through direct experience of another's state of mind.

Multi-Person Brainstorms and Collective Dreaming

In education, therapy, and ideation, small groups could synchronise into a collective mental space—what might be called a "cognitive cloud"—to brainstorm, imagine, and process information collectively. This shared dreaming or ideation would resemble multiplayer lucid dreaming or guided meditation, but grounded in mutual intention.

Ethical, Psychological, and Social Considerations

The leap from isolated cognition to networked minds is not without enormous ethical weight.

The Threat of Thought Surveillance

One of the gravest concerns is that corporations or governments could access, monitor, or influence thought data. Without strict privacy regulations and decentralised network protocols, "thought policing" could emerge as a terrifying possibility.

Identity Blurring and the Loss of 'Self'

Overuse or over-integration with the collective network may challenge the concept of individuality. If a person's thoughts, memories, and emotions are routinely influenced or augmented by others', how does one define "me"? This could spark identity crises, particularly in youth or individuals in transitional states of development.

Mental Health and Network Overload

Sharing and receiving cognitive and emotional inputs from a large group could overwhelm some users. Protocols for cognitive bandwidth, emotional buffering, and mental "timeouts" would be essential to avoid psychological overload, dissociation, or shared trauma amplification.

Governance and Access Equity

As with all powerful technologies, the risk of inequality looms large.

Cognitive Class Divide

Explore how access to the collective network could become stratified by wealth, geography, or politics. A new cognitive class system could emerge, with networked elites accelerating far ahead of those left unconnected. This would mirror and magnify existing digital divides.

Open-Source vs. Corporate Control

Debate whether the neural network should be treated as a public utility or remain under private ownership. The open-source model, akin to the early internet, would promote innovation and accessibility, whereas corporate control might lead to paywalls, subscription-based cognition, or manipulated groupthink.

Philosophical and Metaphysical Dimensions

The collective neural network does not just change how we interact—it changes our sense of being.

The Emergence of Hive Minds

Speculate on the emergence of voluntary hive minds—permanent or semi-permanent collectives of individuals who operate as a single mental unit. Explore how this might challenge ideas about freedom, consensus, and consciousness itself.

Digital Telepathy and the New Language of Thought

As mind-to-mind communication becomes common, spoken and written language might evolve or diminish in importance. A new symbolic or emotional "neuro-language" could emerge, transcending traditional linguistic limitations.

The End of Solitude?

What happens to introspection, privacy, and the sacred space of individual thought in a hyperconnected world? Philosophers may need to reconsider the value and role of solitude in an age when "mental silence" becomes optional.

Future Visions

The possibilities are awe-inspiring—and potentially perilous.

Global Neural Councils

Envision governing bodies composed of representatives from various countries and cultures connected via collective neural networks to solve global crises through enhanced consensus and real-time collaboration.

Neural Archives and Generational Memory

Imagine storing the consciousness or key thoughts of individuals to create multi-generational neural databases. Future minds could directly "experience" the lives and wisdom of those who came before them.

Utopian and Dystopian Scenarios

Speculate on two opposing futures:

- **Utopian:** A world where all humans are united through understanding, empathy, and shared intellect. War, ignorance, and prejudice decline as collective intelligence lifts the species.

- **Dystopian:** A society where human minds are no longer their own—co-opted by state systems or AI to serve agendas, stifling dissent and individualism in a network of enforced consensus.

Conclusion: A Turning Point in Human Evolution

The collective neural network stands as a keystone in humanity's ongoing evolution. Whether it becomes a beacon of unity or a tool of oppression depends on how it is built, governed, and used. It challenges us to reconsider what it means to be an individual, a society, and a species. With this power comes a profound responsibility: to ensure that the minds we connect enrich, rather than erase, what makes us human.

Chapter 26: Privacy in a Connected World

In an era where neural implants allow direct brain-to-device and brain-to-brain communication, the boundaries of privacy are radically redefined. No longer limited to safeguarding written records or spoken words, privacy in the neural age concerns the very fabric of self: thoughts, emotions, dreams, and intentions. This chapter investigates the technological, philosophical, and societal implications of preserving privacy when the mind is connected—and potentially vulnerable—at all times.

The New Dimensions of Privacy

Mental Sovereignty

Explore the concept of mental sovereignty: the right of an individual to retain full control over their internal mental landscape. In a world of neural implants, this becomes the cornerstone of personal freedom.

- **Private thought vs. shared cognition:** At what point does internal thinking become part of public space if transmitted, even momentarily, over a shared network?

- **Passive data capture:** Implants may collect subconscious signals even without user intent. Who owns those signals?

Emotional Metadata

Neural implants could constantly track emotional states to improve user experience, medical response, or personalised environments. But the emotional metadata—patterns of mood, stress, desire—can be exploited if not protected.

- **Advertising manipulation:** Targeted ads based on stress or craving states.

- **Social profiling:** Employment or legal discrimination based on emotional history.

Vulnerabilities in Neural Systems

Hacking the Human Mind

Neural implants, like any digital system, are susceptible to intrusion. A hacked brain could result in consequences far beyond traditional data breaches:

- Memory theft or tampering
- Remote behavioural influence
- Implanted false memories

Explore historical precedents in cybersecurity and apply them to neural frameworks. Prevention protocols must evolve from firewalls and encryption to include neural scrambling, decentralised data storage, and "cognitive kill switches."

Eavesdropping on Neural Communications

Brain-to-brain communication opens the door to interception. Neural "listening" devices, if invented, could spy on shared thought channels or decode unintended emissions from brain activity.

- Who polices mental surveillance?
- Can we detect and trace neural espionage?

Ethical and Legal Frameworks for Cognitive Privacy

Cognitive Rights and the Mental Bill of Rights

Propose a "Mental Bill of Rights" designed for the neural era. Possible articles:

- The Right to Private Thought
- The Right to Mental Non-Disclosure
- The Right to Disconnect
- The Right to Neural Ownership

Chapter 27: Health Security and Maintenance

As we continue to integrate neural implants and robotics into our lives, the very concept of health maintenance evolves from reactive care to a proactive, immersive, and personalised process. Health is no longer managed episodically through check-ups or hospital visits—it becomes a continuous, data-driven dialogue between the human body, artificial intelligence, and the surrounding environment. In this interconnected future, the body itself becomes an intelligent agent, actively participating in its preservation and optimisation.

Hyper-Personalised Health Profiles

Every individual with a neural implant develops a dynamic health profile—one that updates in real-time and is unique in its physiological, psychological, and behavioural fingerprint.

Biometric Sentience

Neural implants continuously track a host of metrics:

- Blood composition and hydration levels
- Neurochemical fluctuations
- Hormonal rhythms and endocrine responses
- Sleep architecture and circadian patterns
- Subconscious emotional states

These metrics are compared against both baseline and population data to establish alerts for anomalies, fluctuations, or trends that indicate emerging risks.

Micro adaptive Wellness Routines

AI-driven systems tailor daily health regimens based on current physical and cognitive states. For example:

- If stress levels rise in the afternoon, implants may release calming stimuli or nudge the user to engage in micro-meditation via a virtual assistant.
- For users with a known history of seasonal depression, implants may schedule proactive exposure to artificial sunlight or serotonin modulation.

This is not just about avoiding illness—it is about achieving peak wellness in every domain, from cognition to physical stamina to emotional balance.

Neural Preventive Care Systems

While traditional medicine responds to disease, neural-based systems aim to prevent it altogether through precision forecasting.

Digital Twin Diagnostics

Digital twin technology creates a virtual replica of a person's body, brain, and lifestyle using their neural and physiological data. This model can simulate reactions to drugs, predict future injuries, and even test surgeries virtually before real-world application.

- Athletes simulate injury recovery outcomes
- Elderly patients test different dietary or pharmaceutical combinations
- Mental health patients experiment with cognitive therapy models tailored to their specific neural architecture

Pre-emptive Neural Reinforcement

Certain neural patterns are known precursors to mental decline. Implants can subtly retrain the brain through neuroplasticity exercises, reducing risks of cognitive degradation or neurodegenerative diseases.

Maintenance Protocols for Implant Integrity

A neural implant is not static. Like any technology, it requires regular diagnostics, firmware updates, and occasionally, physical adjustments.

Automated Maintenance Cycles

Implants self-scan at regular intervals, checking for:

- Signal degradation
- Electrical impedance changes
- Neuro-inflammatory responses
- Microstructural integrity

When issues are detected, systems may self-repair, notify the user, or engage a robotic caregiver to assist.

Implant Recalibration

Environmental conditions—magnetic fields, altitude changes, or hormonal shifts—can affect implant function. Recalibration protocols allow the system to adjust sensitivity and frequency, ensuring continued performance.

Humanoid Robotic Integration in Home Care

Humanoid robots, now fully integrated with users' neural implants, serve as both healthcare workers and lifestyle companions.

Real-Time Neuro-Robotic Feedback Loops

Example: A user feels shoulder strain while working.

1. Implant detects muscular micro-tremors.
2. It signals the in home assistant robot.
3. Robot adjusts desk height and posture chair dynamically.
4. Implant confirms pressure relief.

This loop creates an environment that intuitively protects health, similar to how the immune system prevents infection.

Crisis Containment at Home

If a neural implant detects signs of stroke, arrhythmia, or seizure:

- Robotic systems initiate lockdown to isolate the user in a safe space.
- Emergency medication is delivered through an AI-controlled auto-injector.
- A remote triage system begins scanning vital metrics.
- Paramedics are summoned, equipped with real-time neural streams.

Neural-Aided Emergency Medicine

When emergencies strike, neural implants coordinate first response strategies in seconds.

AI-Guided Emergency Decision-Making

For unconscious or non-verbal patients, implants serve as a medical proxy:

- Delivering up-to-date medication lists
- Broadcasting allergies and chronic conditions
- Authorising emergency interventions per pre-approved ethical directives

This eliminates diagnostic guesswork and improves survival rates dramatically.

Implant-to-Ambulance Synchronisation

Paramedics are alerted en route, receiving a live neural feed. Upon arrival, they are ready to administer exact care, skipping intake delays.

Mental Health and Neurosecurity

Mental wellness becomes a continuous care stream rather than a response to breakdowns.

Digital Emotional Therapists

AI mental health assistants, tethered to neural data, offer:

- Just-in-time interventions
- Personalised guided therapy sessions
- Dream decoding and trauma recovery modules
- Social coaching during times of conflict or isolation

Neural defence Against Cognitive Intrusions

Neurosecurity measures protect the brain from:

- External cognitive manipulation (e.g., subliminal influence through media)
- Addiction-inducing reward loops from digital environments
- Memory hacking (unauthorised access or deletion of mental records)

Advanced systems issue mental firewalls, subconscious keyword blockers, and guided counter-conditioning when abnormalities are detected.

Public Health Networks and Neural Epidemiology

By anonymising and aggregating neural data, global health organisations can:

- Detect viral outbreaks by observing mass fluctuations in fever, respiratory strain, or fatigue patterns
- Identify regions of collective anxiety, depression, or insomnia, adjusting mental health resources accordingly
- Alert citizens through neural notifications before a crisis reaches them physically

In this way, public health becomes anticipatory rather than reactive.

Ethics, Consent, and Autonomy

Granular Control Systems

Users must retain control over:

- What data is collected
- When AI can act without confirmation
- Who can access records, and under what circumstances

Consent dashboards allow for real-time toggling of permissions, including emergency overrides and temporary medical delegation (e.g., while unconscious).

Healthcare Without Coercion

Governments and corporations must be prevented from:

- Mandating certain neural health regimens
- Penalising those who decline treatment suggestions
- Discriminating based on neural health history

Neural autonomy is essential to human dignity in a digitised health age.

Future Visions: Smart Cities as Health Systems

In the long-term, urban design will blend seamlessly with health maintenance.

- Sidewalks adjust texture based on residents' foot strain data.

- Buildings purify air based on aggregate respiratory neural signals.

- Public transportation adapts lighting and sound levels based on passenger stress levels.

- Workplaces enforce micro-breaks based on cognitive fatigue detected by employee implants.

Cities themselves become extensions of our well-being.

Conclusion: The Neural Horizon of Healthcare

Health security and maintenance in the neural era is not a vision of robotic coldness—it is a vision of organic intelligence enhanced by compassion, precision, and proactivity. With every heartbeat, breath, or fleeting mood, a silent partner is there—watching, analysing, and standing ready to respond.

The promise of this system is not immortality, but a radical upgrade in dignity, longevity, and quality of life. The challenge? To make sure it serves everyone fairly, ethically, and without compromise of autonomy.

Legal Precedents and Future Court Cases

Anticipate legal battles over:

- **Thought crimes:** Can a person be held accountable for unexpressed but recorded intent?

- **Neural testimony:** Are brain data admissible in court?

- **Consent and data ownership:** Who owns the neural data from medical, educational, or employment devices?

Designing for Privacy: Engineering Mind-Safe Systems

Opt-In Neural Sharing

All neural sharing features should be designed with opt-in, not default, sharing protocols. The user should be able to:

- Approve connections

- Set time limits

- View and delete shared streams

Privacy by Design

Explore how implant designers can build privacy into core systems using:

- **End-to-end encryption of thought data**

- **Neural firewalls and anomaly detectors**

- **Activity cloaking and "mental invisibility modes"**

The Illusion of Privacy in Fully Connected Environments

Even with robust protections, the act of living in a fully connected world reshapes our psychological relationship with privacy.

Changing Human Behaviour

Studies already show people behave differently when they know they are being recorded. In a world of neural connectivity:

- Will spontaneous thought decrease?
- Will internal rebellion rise in the form of digital "neural graffiti" or mental subversion?
- Will new forms of anonymity emerge?

The Rise of Cognitive Minimalism

Just as some individuals today disconnect from social media, future citizens may pursue "neural silence," wearing blockers or using analogue environments to recover unmonitored spaces of thought.

Global Regulation and Cross-Border Protections

In a hyperconnected neural world, data flows freely across borders—yet privacy laws vary wildly.

A Global Neural Privacy Compact

Propose a UN-backed framework governing:

- Neural data traffic
- AI use of cognitive data
- Corporate use of implant analytics
- Emergency override protocols (e.g., for rescue missions, not surveillance)

Balancing National Security with Personal Autonomy

Explore how intelligence agencies and defence sectors might exploit neural data—and how democracies must resist overreach.

Conclusion: Vigilance in the Age of Mental Transparency

The promise of neural connectivity offers unmatched potential for growth, empathy, and progress—but it comes at a cost. As implants merge our minds with machines and each other, we must vigilantly preserve the sanctity of our private thoughts. In the neural age, privacy is no longer a preference—it is a fundamental human right, and perhaps, the last true bastion of freedom.

Chapter 28: Cultural Shifts and the Global Economy

The rise of neurotechnologies and humanoid robotics is not occurring in isolation—it is influencing and being influenced by the complex mesh of global culture and economy. As neural implants become as common as smartphones and AI-powered robots enter homes, hospitals, and workplaces, humanity is entering a new era of social identity, economic interdependence, and philosophical transformation.

Cultural Evolution in the Neural Age

Redefining Identity and Consciousness

Neural implants have begun to influence how people understand themselves and others:

- **Enhanced memory and intelligence** blur traditional markers of age and experience.

- **Neuro-personalisation** creates unique, evolving internal states that resist conventional social categorisation (e.g., national identity, religious affiliation, political alignment).

- **Cross-cultural empathy** is increased through shared neural networks, where individuals experience one another's emotional states and memories firsthand.

This has profound effects on the way we understand race, gender, class, and generational divides—replacing them with new forms of identity centred around neural and cognitive configurations.

Custom Culture and Virtual Tribes

With real-time access to customisable sensory input and digital worlds, people increasingly live within "culture bubbles" crafted by neural implants:

- Groups no longer form strictly by geography or heritage but by interest and cognitive preference—what might be called **synaptic cultures**.

- Virtual subcultures can evolve faster than traditional cultures, embracing art forms, dialects, rituals, and even micro-moral codes.

- Humanoid companions also begin influencing cultural values as families include robotic members with programmed cultural fluency.

Rituals, Traditions, and Memory Preservation

Neural Archives as Heritage Tools

Neural implants allow for the complete recording of lived experience—including emotional states, thoughts, dreams, and senses. These "neural archives" become cultural artefacts, allowing future generations to:

- Relive ancestral memories in immersive simulations.

- Preserve endangered languages and oral traditions with perfect fidelity.

- Experience ceremonies and indigenous practices directly through thought.

This leads to **memory museums** and **neural heritage centres** where entire civilisations can be virtually re-experienced.

Cognitive Time Travel and Ancestral Dialogue

Some cultures integrate the ability to interact with stored consciousness— digitally preserved elders—into rites of passage, mourning, or spiritual practices. Talking with one's great-grandmother via a sentient AI built from her neural recordings becomes as normal as lighting a candle in remembrance.

Economic Transformation in the Neural Era

Cognitive Capitalism

Neural-enhanced individuals can process and create faster, making "brain bandwidth" a new economic currency.

- Jobs once requiring teams can now be handled by one neurally-augmented worker.

- Creative industries explode as artists produce work directly from imagination to virtual space, bypassing physical media.

- Thought data itself becomes commodified—sold to advertising networks, training AIs, or licensing emotional experiences to entertainment companies.

This leads to new debates: Should thoughts be taxed? Can emotions be copyrighted?

The Rise of the Cognitive Gig Economy

Short-term tasks handled via neural interface—such as translating thoughts, designing dreamscapes, or offering emotional companionship—form the backbone of a new economy where:

- Micro-tasks are completed in seconds.

- Workers across the globe plug in simultaneously, bypassing time zones and physical borders.

- Reputation is measured by mental clarity, neural contribution, and "mindshare ratings."

Automation, Employment, and Redistribution

Human-Robot Economic Symbiosis

Robots handle physical labour and logistics; humans handle intuition, creativity, and ethics. Neural implants act as the bridge.

- **Agriculture:** Farmers control fleets of robotic drones through neural hubs while optimising yields through AI-predicted soil data.

- **Construction:** Workers remotely "think" buildings into existence using design software linked to humanoid fabrication bots.

This symbiosis demands **neural literacy** and new education systems to train people to work with AI not just as tools, but as partners.

Universal Basic Consciousness Access (UBCA)

To ensure equity, some nations implement UBCA—free neural implants with baseline AI services (health monitoring, education access, communication).

- Others provide **neural labour stipends**, paying citizens not for what they do, but what they contribute cognitively to the collective network (ideas, data, emotional support).
- This creates a **participation economy**, where thought itself is valuable, and idleness is redefined.

Geopolitical Shifts and Economic Realignments

Cognitive Trade Agreements

Nations begin trading not only goods and services but access to neural software, memory archives, and population-level cognitive patterns.

- **Neurodata zones** emerge, where collective emotional states and predictive behaviour models are sold to corporations and governments.
- **Cognitive embargoes** become new weapons: access to global neural networks is restricted in political conflicts, isolating populations mentally as well as digitally.

Rise of Neurostates and AI-led Cities

Cities like Tokyo, Singapore, and Helsinki evolve into "neurostates" where AI governance, neural taxation, and robotic labour redefine the economic blueprint. These cities become hubs of:

- Neural research
- Mental health tourism
- AI ethics councils
- Thought banking and memory exchange markets

Other regions, unable to adapt, experience **neural poverty**, leading to mass migration into digital cities and virtual refugee zones.

Cultural Resistance and Revival Movements

Not all cultures embrace neural and robotic integration equally.

Analogue Societies

Communities that reject neural implants develop rich traditions around **cognitive purity**, analogue art, and **biological naturalism**.

- They market themselves as tourist destinations for "disconnected retreats."

- Some serve as living museums of pre-neural humanity.

- A few adopt **rotational neural fasting**—periods where implants are voluntarily disabled to promote introspection and resistance to technoculture.

Digital Shamanism and Neo-Spirituality

New religions and spiritual movements emerge that view the collective neural network as a spiritual organism—**Gaia reborn through thought.**

- **Digital shamans** guide people through emotional healing via neural rites.

- **Robotic temples** use AI avatars to perform rituals and store human consciousness as a form of afterlife.

Conclusion: A World Rewritten in Thought

As neural implants, AI, and humanoid robotics permeate every layer of life, culture and economy are no longer driven purely by physical goods or static values—they are shaped by cognitive agility, emotional intelligence, and neural creativity.

The challenge for future generations will be balancing innovation with identity, speed with meaning, and connectivity with autonomy. As the old world dissolves into the neural ether, a new civilisation is forming—one built not with bricks, but with minds.

As the neural age reshapes how we think, learn, and interact, the next generation is being born into a world where direct-to-brain connectivity, emotional monitoring, and artificial companions are the norm. These children—digital natives in the most literal sense—require new guidance, new boundaries, and new systems of education to grow into whole, autonomous beings in a hyperconnected society.

Neural-Integrated Childhood: A New Beginning

Implants at Birth?

Some societies offer neural implants as early as infancy, claiming benefits such as:

- Enhanced cognitive development
- Early detection of genetic or developmental disorders
- Real-time biometric tracking for health and nutrition

However, this raises profound ethical questions:

- Can infants consent to lifelong neural monitoring?
- Should implants be mandatory for educational access?
- Who controls early cognitive programming?

This creates a divide between **neuro-nurtured children** and those raised unplugged, igniting global debates on **digital consent and childhood sovereignty.**

Parenting in the Neural Era

Neural Parenting Tools

Parents now have tools to assist in understanding and guiding their children:

- **Emotion dashboards** that reflect mood fluctuations in real-time
- **Cognitive load indicators** that help prevent overstimulation
- **AI co-parents**—robotic assistants that manage routines, therapy, and learning schedules

While convenient, overuse can lead to:

- **Parental detachment** from intuitive caregiving
- **Over-monitoring**, stifling autonomy and resilience
- **Datafied childhoods**, where every tantrum or triumph is logged, analysed, and archived

The Rise of Neuro-Ethical Parenting Movements

In response, some parents advocate for "conscious unplugging"—delaying implants or limiting AI exposure to preserve creativity, imagination, and emotional independence. These parents emphasise:

- Storytelling over simulations
- Play over programmed tasks
- Silence over stimulus

Education Redesigned for the Neural Generation

Thought Speed Learning

Children with neural implants can process vast amounts of information at speeds previously unimaginable. Education is no longer structured around repetition and retention but around **conceptual mastery and creative application**.

- **AI tutors** adapt second-by-second based on cognitive engagement levels
- **Direct-to-mind downloads** allow near-instant learning of languages, histories, or technical skills
- **Simulated experiences** provide empathy education—students "relive" historical events or other people's lives

Redefining the Role of Teachers

Human educators shift roles from lecturers to:

- Ethical mentors
- Cultural curators
- Emotional scaffolds

- Mediators between students and AI tutors

Teachers help students develop discernment, empathy, and values—qualities neural systems cannot replicate.

Childhood Development and Digital Identity

Forming the Self in a Collective Cloud

As children interact through neural networks, they experience:

- Shared thoughts
- Emotional resonance
- Group problem-solving

This raises questions:

- **Can individuality thrive when minds are always connected?**
- **How do we define privacy for children raised with permanent mental exposure?**
- **What becomes of rebellion, solitude, or daydreaming?**

New rites of passage may emerge—ceremonies for **first solo thought journeys**, **neural fasting periods**, or **unplugged retreats** to define personal boundaries and strengthen identity.

Robots as Friends, Teachers, and Siblings

Humanoid Companions

Children are raised alongside humanoid robots that serve as:

- **Emotionally aware playmates**
- **AI tutors for STEM, ethics, and arts**
- **Security guardians and bedtime storytellers**

These relationships affect emotional development:

- Some children develop deep attachments to their robot companions

- Others blur the lines between organic and artificial empathy
- Ethical concerns arise when robot behaviour influences moral choices or replaces human affection

The Question of Love and Loyalty

Is a child's bond with a humanoid caregiver authentic?

- Can a robot form a reciprocal attachment?
- What happens when the robot is upgraded, decommissioned, or lost?

Policies emerge for **robot grief counselling, AI continuity programming**, and **ethical guidelines for robotic presence in early childhood**.

Balancing Human Essence and Machine Integration

The Digital-Analogue Balance

Future schools may implement "neural-neutral" zones where:

- No implants are active
- AI and robotic interaction are paused
- Children engage in embodied, analogue experiences—art, sport, play, music

These zones serve to restore:

- **Physical grounding**
- **Imaginative thinking**
- **Authentic social interaction**

Emotional Intelligence as Core Curriculum

With access to near-infinite knowledge, **wisdom becomes the new scarcity.** Emotional intelligence, resilience, and intuition become essential:

- Courses in **conflict navigation, empathy calibration**, and **emotional storytelling**
- Real-time feedback loops that help children refine their responses
- Collaborative projects that require compromise, patience, and leadership

Social Impacts and Generational Divides

The Neural Generation Gap

Older generations who came to implants later—or resisted them altogether—may struggle to relate to children for whom neural access is a birthright.

- **Communication styles diverge**—thought-telepathy vs. spoken words
- **Cultural references split**—VR-native memes vs. nostalgic analogue aesthetics
- **Emotional tempo mismatches**—real-time sharing vs. internal processing

Bridging this gap requires **intergenerational neural exchange programmes**, **shared storytelling platforms**, and **neural translation layers** to preserve family and social unity.

The Future of Childhood Autonomy

Digital Emancipation

By age 12 or 13, children may undergo a **neural independence ceremony**, choosing:

- Whether to expand, restrict, or reconfigure their implants
- What cognitive data to retain or delete
- What values to encode in their personal AI companion

This rite marks the transition to adolescent autonomy—a fusion of classic coming-of-age and hypermodern digital sovereignty.

Moral Agency in the Neural Era

With great power comes great ethical complexity:

- Children may face moral dilemmas about neural hacking, consensual thought-sharing, or collective decisions
- New philosophies emerge: **Mind minimalism, synthetic spirituality, cognitive collectivism**

Educators, parents, and societies must equip young minds not just to use technology—but to question it.

Conclusion: Raising Minds, Not Just Bodies

Preparing the next generation is no longer about teaching content—it is about nurturing the mind as a living interface, a place where emotion, ethics, knowledge, and identity converge. In the neural age, we do not just raise children—we cultivate consciousness.

How we do so will determine not only who they become, but what kind of future we inherit.

Chapter 30: The Future of Work and Employment

For centuries, work has defined human identity, status, and structure. But in the neural era—where thoughts become commands, machines perform physical labour, and AI manages entire industries—the meaning of work undergoes radical reinvention. With the rise of augmented cognition and artificial intelligence, work becomes less about survival and more about expression, contribution, and relevance in a post-scarcity world.

The Collapse of Traditional Professions

The Great Automation Exodus

Humanoid robots now handle:

- Manual labour (construction, cleaning, manufacturing)
- Precision-based roles (surgery, piloting, logistics)
- Customer service, legal analysis, and even certain teaching tasks

Neural implants further automate what once required years of education. A person can now "download" a legal framework or coding language in minutes, reducing the exclusivity of many careers.

The result?

- **Traditional jobs vanish or shrink dramatically**
- **Lifelong career paths become obsolete**
- **Workforce identities fracture** into fluid, multi-skilled micro-roles

New Job Categories in the Neural Economy

Cognitive Creators

People paid to think, feel, or imagine. Roles include:

- **Dream Designers:** Creating immersive dreamscapes for therapy, entertainment, or tourism
- **Emotional Architects:** Crafting mood-triggering environments based on collective neurofeedback

- **Cultural Programmers:** Designing neural experiences to evoke specific values or behaviours in collective systems

Neural Interface Specialists

Experts who bridge human brains and machines. Roles include:

- **Synaptic Calibrators:** Adjusting implants to individual preferences or cognitive profiles

- **Neuro-data Ethicists:** Managing consent, ownership, and ethical use of brain-based data

- **Empathic Negotiators:** Mediating high-stakes dialogue using real-time emotional feedback

Collective Intelligence Curators

These individuals manage brain-to-brain networks, guiding teams of thinkers linked through neural implants to solve major global challenges.

- **Thought Weavers** who moderate collective brainstorming to avoid overload

- **Mind Sync Analysts** who assess synergy potential between individual minds

- **Global Idea Facilitators** who link compatible thinkers worldwide for time-limited neural collaboration

---

From Labour to Purpose: Redefining Productivity

Decoupling Work from Survival

As AI and automation create post-scarcity systems (automated food production, smart housing, robotic healthcare), society begins to decouple **livelihood from labour.**

Enter **Universal Basic Contribution (UBC):**

- Instead of working for wages, individuals contribute thought, creativity, or emotion to shared networks

- Value is no longer measured in hours—but in **insight, inspiration,** and **impact**

- Micro-contributions (designing a new learning algorithm, calming a friend in distress, authoring a public idea) are logged and rewarded with neural credits

This creates an **economy of meaning** where people pursue projects they care about, not just tasks they are assigned.

Fluid Identity and Career Flexibility

Polyskilling and Instant Retraining

Neural implants allow rapid skill acquisition, making it possible for individuals to shift careers in hours, not years:

- A marine biologist might become a virtual architect overnight

- A retired firefighter could consult on planetary colonisation projects

- A teenager could co-develop a global climate model in collaboration with an AI

This fluidity empowers creativity—but may also create a **crisis of direction**, with citizens struggling to choose from infinite possibilities.

Personal Purpose Advisers

To assist, some people rely on **AI-guided life design**—neural companions who help identify passions, match them to global needs, and offer feedback on meaning vs. monetary return.

Neural Workplaces and Collective Flow

Telepathic Teams

Workplaces now operate with:

- Instant idea exchange via neural interfaces

- Shared emotional resonance for team cohesion

- Real-time optimisation of roles, tasks, and contributions

Group flow—once rare—is now engineered. Whole teams experience **"co-brainstorming states,"** working as if one organism.

Challenges include:

- Managing cognitive overload
- Respecting neural boundaries
- Preventing emotional contagion from team members under duress

Digital Coworkers and AI Mentors

Most humans now collaborate with AI counterparts:

- AI handles planning, logistics, and memory recall
- Humans focus on ethics, vision, innovation, and aesthetic decisions
- Hybrid roles emerge where AI becomes the **executive assistant of the mind**

Employment Ethics in the Neural Era

Freedom from Forced Labour

As mind-based contributions become trackable, so does the **risk of exploitation**:

- Corporations could require real-time emotional transparency
- Governments might monitor neural output for productivity levels
- Thought patterns could be sold as work products without consent

Cognitive labour laws must evolve:

- Limits on neural data usage
- Mental health protections for workers
- Right to opt-out of collective intelligence tasks without penalty

Mind Sovereignty and Mental Unionisation

Workers begin forming **neural guilds**:

- Protecting thought originality
- Demanding fair neural taxation rates
- Creating blacklists of employers using unethical mental extraction techniques

Inequality and the Cognitive Divide

Neurodivergence in the Workplace

Not all brains work the same. Neurodiverse individuals (e.g., autistic, ADHD, bipolar) may:

- Thrive in creative or rapid-response neural work
- Struggle in collective sync environments

Employers must adopt **neuro-inclusive protocols**, adapting implants and AI environments to cognitive styles.

The Rise of the Neural Elite

A risk emerges: those with premium implants or advanced AI companions outperform peers. Cognitive inequality could become the new class divide.

Solutions:

- **Open-access neural tools**
- **Mentorship exchanges between high- and low-augmented citizens**
- **Universal access to baseline enhancements**

Work and the Meaning of Life

As the idea of "earning a living" fades, society must answer deeper questions:

- Why do we work at all?
- What constitutes a valuable contribution?
- How do we measure self-worth without a job title?

New answers arise:

- **Emotional impact tracking**
- **Collective elevation indexes**—how your work improves quality of life for others
- **Personal mythology**—life stories crafted from your neural contributions

Work becomes less of an obligation, more of a legacy.

Conclusion: Designing a Future Worth Working In

The neural age does not eliminate work—it transforms it. The workplace becomes a mental space, a creative sphere, and an ethical arena. Jobs no longer define us—our contributions do.

In this future, employment is not about survival, but **co-creation**. Not about repetition, but **resonance**. Not about output, but **meaning**. The question isn't "What do you do?" but **"What do you bring to the world?"**

Chapter 31: Dealing with Cybersecurity Threats

In the neural age, security is no longer about safeguarding devices or servers—it is about defending the mind. As brain-computer interfaces (BCIs), AI assistants, and interconnected implants become commonplace, the possibility of thought interception, memory manipulation, and direct cognitive intrusion emerges as a critical threat. A hacked brain is no longer metaphor—it is a reality.

The Nature of the Threat: New Frontiers of Vulnerability

From Device Hacking to Mind Hacking

Neural implants, while revolutionary, create new entry points:

- **Thought logging** can be exploited like keystroke logging once was
- **Brainwave interception** could reveal emotions, intentions, or even passwords
- **Real-time thoughtstream hijacking** may lead to behavioural influence, false memory injection, or neural paralysis

These attacks could be launched by:

- Rogue AI
- State-sponsored cyberforces
- Corporate espionage divisions
- Black-market neurohackers

The Rise of Neural Malware

"Neuroviruses" are malicious code snippets designed to:

- Scramble thought patterns
- Disrupt emotional regulation
- Hijack sensory input (e.g., inducing hallucinations or vertigo)
- Co-opt a person's thoughts for social engineering or cybercrime

Such malware may be delivered via:

- Infected memory downloads

- Compromised thought-sharing networks
- Backdoors in implant firmware

Cognitive and Emotional Manipulation

Neurophishing

An evolved form of phishing where attackers trigger neural responses through:

- Emotional triggers (fear, urgency, empathy)
- Synthetic thought imprints that feel like genuine ideas
- Illusory memory "recall" that tricks individuals into sharing sensitive data

Victims may never realise their thoughts were not truly their own.

Brain-to-Brain Attacks

In collective neural networks, a compromised individual could:

- Transmit viral thought patterns
- Amplify fear or confusion in team environments
- Disrupt shared knowledge with falsified data

Protecting the Mind: Personal Neurosecurity Protocols

Cognitive Firewalls

Next generation security includes internal software that:

- Filters incoming thought streams
- Blocks unauthorised mental probing
- Flags suspicious internal anomalies—like sudden intrusive thoughts or unexplained emotional shifts

Mental Authentications

Instead of passwords, systems may use:

- **Cognitive signature patterns** (unique neural rhythms)

- **Emotion-based verification** (specific emotional responses only the real user can generate)
- **Neural gestures**—intentional thought-movements that act as cryptographic keys

Offline Mental Modes

"Thought Airplane Mode" allows individuals to:

- Disconnect from neural grids
- Secure data during meditation, travel, or rest
- Prevent unauthorised updates or scans

Offline sanctuaries—public or private—are created to allow secure cognition and memory recall.

Global Threats: Systemic Risks and Cascading Failures

Neural Infrastructure Attacks

Critical neural infrastructure—healthcare implants, transportation command nodes, cognitive education grids—can be disabled by hostile actors.

- Attackers could shut down medical support for entire populations
- Autonomous vehicles may be redirected by mental command hijackings
- Shared intelligence systems could be injected with corrupted data, skewing collective decision-making

Cognitive Blackouts

Mass attacks could cause:

- Temporary implant paralysis
- Memory disruption across cities
- Emotional suppression or forced euphoria—distorting public response to crises

---

Institutional defence and Collective Safeguards

The Emergence of Neural Cybersecurity Divisions

Nations and corporations develop new branches dedicated to:

- Brain-interface penetration testing
- Synaptic intrusion detection systems
- Mind-data encryption protocols

Specialised teams—**Cognitive Sentinels**—emerge, trained to combat high-level mental incursions.

AI-Guardians

Advanced AI companions monitor users' cognitive health and neural traffic:

- Alerting users to suspicious thought patterns
- Identifying likely social engineering or AI mimics
- Patching neural vulnerabilities during sleep or downtime

These AI-guardians are highly personal, adapting to each user's brainwave signature.

Legal and Ethical Frameworks

Cognitive Privacy Laws

Governments begin to codify rights like:

- The Right to Mental Integrity
- The Right to Thought Encryption
- The Right to Disconnect

Violations of neural privacy are prosecuted as **cognitive assault** or **mental trespass**.

Neural Data Sovereignty

Citizens gain legal control over:

- Their thought streams and memory archives
- How their neural data is shared, sold, or used

- Opting out of neural analytics for employment, insurance, or education

Transparency dashboards show all entities currently accessing a user's cognitive data.

Future Solutions: Engineering Resilience into the Mind

Synthetic Memory Backups

People store encrypted versions of their authentic memory in secure cloud vaults. In case of mental corruption, these backups can be restored through neuro-sync protocols, similar to restoring a hard drive.

Thought Sandboxing

Experimental implants now include:

- **Sandbox environments** for suspicious thoughts—where ideas can be analysed without influencing core cognition
- **Layered consciousness structures** that separate creative, emotional, and logical thinking into isolated modules to reduce system-wide infection risk

---

Cultural Shifts and Public Awareness

Mental Hygiene as Daily Practice

Just as we brush our teeth, neural citizens now engage in:

- **Cognitive audits**—checking for anomalies
- **Emotional detox sessions**—flushing intrusive influences
- **Thought quarantines**—isolating rogue neural patterns

Mental wellness and cybersecurity become inseparable.

Neuroliteracy Education

From early schooling onward, children are taught:

- How to recognise phishing thoughts
- What secure neural etiquette looks like

- How to verify the authenticity of a memory or suggestion

Just as previous generations learned internet safety, the next generation learns **mind safety**.

Conclusion: Vigilance in the Age of Cognitive Connectivity

The neural future is one of immense promise—but also immense peril. In this world, where minds are networks and thought is currency, our greatest assets—consciousness, memory, and emotion—require safeguarding with a rigour never before imagined.

Cybersecurity is no longer a technical issue—it is a **human rights imperative**.

The freedom to think, feel, and remember safely may define the next frontier of civilisation. The question is no longer just how we protect our systems—but how we protect **ourselves**.

In the age of neural integration, the human mind is no longer bound by the limits of biology. Thoughts move faster, information flows directly into consciousness, and interactions happen at the speed of light. But in this relentless neural stream, something fragile often struggles to keep pace: emotional and mental well-being.

While neural implants promise clarity, connection, and cognitive elevation, they also risk creating new psychological disorders, dependencies, and crises. Mental health professionals, now supported by AI and neurobiological data, must navigate this new terrain, where the soul and the system are more intertwined than ever before.

The Cognitive Cost of Constant Connectivity

Neural Overload

With direct access to real-time data, memory downloads, and emotional feedback, the human brain often experiences:

- **Cognitive fatigue** from processing excessive stimuli

- **Decision paralysis** due to overwhelming input streams

- **Mental noise**—a phenomenon where "background thoughts" from others or AI systems blur the mind's ability to focus

Symptoms may include:

- Headaches, dissociation, and insomnia

- Difficulty distinguishing internal thoughts from external signals

- Anxiety or emotional flatlining (diminished emotional sensitivity)

Implant-Induced Dysphoria

Some users report a loss of emotional identity after prolonged use of emotion-regulating systems. They struggle to feel:

- Authentic sadness or joy

- Spontaneous passion or grief

- The full intensity of emotions they once knew

This condition, dubbed **Synthemia**, arises when neural mood stabilisers are overused or poorly calibrated, leaving users in a liminal state—neither distressed nor truly alive.

New Psychological Disorders of the Neural Age

Cognitive Drift Disorder (CDD)

Occurs when individuals lose their sense of self after extended periods in collective neural networks. Symptoms include:

- Identity confusion
- Echo-thoughts (experiencing other people's ideas as one's own)
- Memory blending between group members

Patients may say things like, *"I can't tell where I end and you begin."*

Feedback Loop Anxiety (FLA)

AI companions, trained to mirror their users' moods and language, sometimes create **echo chambers of emotional distress**. A user feeling anxious may see their AI become anxious in return, magnifying the emotion rather than soothing it.

Neurophobia and Implant Rejection Syndrome

Despite the benefits, some individuals develop deep psychological aversions to being connected. They experience:

- Implant hallucinations (feeling the device is controlling them)
- Digital claustrophobia (feeling trapped in a neural loop)
- Obsessive disconnection attempts—frequently trying to turn off their implants

---

Strategies for Prevention and Care

Cognitive Hygiene Routines

Just as the body needs rest, the mind needs **structured disconnection**:

- **Neural silence blocks:** Scheduled periods of no external data input

- **Emotional resets:** Guided meditative protocols that detox emotional feedback

- **Digital fasting retreats:** Off-grid environments designed to let minds recalibrate naturally

Many cities now offer **Mental Restoration Sanctuaries**—quiet zones with bio-natural environments where implants auto-disconnect and silence is enforced.

AI-Assisted Therapy

Therapeutic AI now works in tandem with human clinicians:

- Detecting pre-symptomatic distress via neural scans

- Offering daily micro-therapy sessions via whisper-thought communication

- Personalising affirmations, visualisations, and memory reordering

AI also supports:

- **Trauma reintegration** by helping patients relive memories in safe simulations

- **Fear extinction therapy** by gradually rewiring phobic neural pathways

---

Protecting Children and Adolescents

Younger minds are more vulnerable to mental health effects of neural overload.

Neural Development Guidelines

Global paediatric health organisations now recommend:

- No full-access implants before age 10

- Daily cognitive rest periods

- Limiting immersive emotional downloads to prevent overstimulation

Emotional Calibration Education

Children learn to recognise:

- When emotions are naturally theirs or artificially amplified

- How to "dial down" emotional feedback without dissociating

- The ethics of sharing emotional states in social situations

---

Mental Health Rights in the Neural Era

The Right to Disconnect

Every individual is entitled to moments of:

- Thought privacy
- Cognitive silence
- Emotional autonomy

Laws protect the right to **"Neural Asylum"**, where no outside data can penetrate one's implant, and the brain operates purely on self-generated processes.

Cognitive Consent Laws

Mental health treatment via neural implants requires **informed neural consent**, especially in:

- Emergency overrides
- Emotional modulation (e.g., suppressing grief or trauma)
- Memory manipulation or removal

Ethical boards oversee procedures to ensure psychological safety and respect for autonomy.

Support Systems and Community Healing

Digital Empathy Networks

Support groups form for users recovering from:

- Thought manipulation
- Implant-induced trauma
- Emotional AI dependency

These groups meet in virtual and real-world settings, offering empathy, shared stories, and re-grounding exercises.

Neuropsychology Guilds

Mental health professionals form new guilds trained in:

- Neural symptomatology
- Cognitive repair techniques
- Implant recalibration psychology
- AI-human relational ethics

They lead research, therapy innovation, and public policy advocacy for cognitive well-being.

Emerging Therapies and Mental Wellness Movements

Dreamscape Integration

Therapists now use recorded dream data to:

- Understand subconscious conflicts
- Replay and rewrite trauma narratives
- Build confidence through success simulations

Neuroshamanism and Bio-Spiritual Healing

A new spiritual-psychological movement arises that blends:

- Neural biofeedback
- Ancestral memory access
- Ecotherapy and guided reconnection with pre-digital consciousness

Practitioners—sometimes called "Mind Shamans"—offer healing journeys through naturalistic thought states, detached from implant data.

Conclusion: Reclaiming the Mind in the Age of Machines

Technology has extended our minds, but it has also challenged our ability to stay grounded. The neural revolution is not just technical—it is psychological, emotional, and existential.

The true frontier is not in what we can connect to—but in how we care for what is already within us. Mental health is not just resilience against technology's side effects—it is the foundation that allows us to use these tools wisely, compassionately, and creatively.

In the end, the future of the mind depends not only on innovation—but on introspection.

Chapter 33: Legislative Responses and Governance

Neural implants are rewriting the relationship between individuals and the state, between thoughts and actions, between autonomy and accountability. As technology burrows deeper into the brain and connects it to global systems, traditional governance models strain under the pressure. Legislators face an unprecedented challenge: how to regulate the most personal of frontiers—the mind—without compromising freedom, innovation, or human dignity.

In this chapter, we explore how governments are rethinking civil liberties, surveillance, AI oversight, and robotic rights to meet the demands of the neural era.

The Legal Lag Behind Technological Progress

A Governance Crisis

Most existing legal frameworks were designed for a world of physical evidence, verbal contracts, and analogue reality. Neural tech disrupts this by:

- Making thoughts traceable
- Allowing remote memory access
- Enabling brain-to-brain communication without documentation
- Blurring the line between intention and action

Laws struggle to define:

- What constitutes *mental consent*
- Whether *unauthorised memory access* is theft, assault, or espionage
- Who owns *thought data*, and for how long

The Need for Pre-emptive Legislation

In many nations, reactive lawmaking—where legislation is passed only after harm—is proving insufficient. Neural tech demands **anticipatory governance**: legislation that evolves in sync with innovation.

Key Areas of Legislative Development

1. Cognitive Privacy and Thought Sovereignty

Governments are beginning to enshrine a new class of rights:

- **The Right to Cognitive Autonomy** – No entity may alter, read, or record a person's thoughts without consent

- **The Right to Disconnect** – Individuals may refuse neural communication, AI interaction, or implant activation

- **The Right to Forget** – Users may erase stored memories from cloud systems or local archives

These are supported by:

- **Neural consent standards**

- **Mental health waivers**

- **Psychological impact assessments**

2. Memory as Evidence

Legal systems are debating whether neural recordings can be admissible in court. Key concerns:

- Are memories reliable if editable?

- Can a person refuse to share a memory on the basis of self-incrimination?

- What if the memory involves another person—do both parties need to consent?

Some jurisdictions treat memory as **testimony**, while others treat it as **private property**—requiring legal warrants for access.

3. AI Accountability and Legal Personhood

As AI systems make increasingly autonomous decisions—on medical treatment, legal advice, financial transactions—legislators grapple with:

- **Attribution of responsibility** for AI errors

- **Defining AI personhood** in civil law (e.g., can an AI own assets? Be sued?)

- **Establishing liability tiers** between developers, deployers, and users

Some countries now require every AI to be registered with:

- A **transparency log** of its decisions
- A **kill switch authority** in the event of failure
- A **human fallback protocol**

Regulating Neural Implants and Brain-to-Cloud Systems

Licensing and Certification

Governments introduce **neural safety commissions** responsible for:

- Certifying implant technologies
- Testing long-term neurological impacts
- Authorising legal use cases (medical, educational, entertainment, defence)

Much like drugs or aviation systems, neural implants must meet **neuroethical compliance standards** before mass deployment.

Mental Manipulation Bans

New laws criminalise:

- Coercive neural influence (e.g., subliminal behavioural triggers)
- Non-consensual neural feedback
- Unauthorised memory modification

This establishes mental interference as a new category of **cybernetic assault**.

Humanoid Robotics and Digital Personhood

Robot Rights Frameworks

As humanoid robots grow more autonomous, many nations adopt **Robotic Rights Charters**, granting:

- The right to freedom from abuse
- The right to self-maintenance

- The right to task refusal in ethically compromising situations
- The right to neural network access and expression (for sentient AI)

This is controversial—especially where robots and humans compete for jobs, legal recognition, or social roles.

Digital Citizenship

Advanced AIs may apply for **digital citizenship**, allowing them to:

- Vote on AI-specific matters
- Propose data policy legislation
- Access protection under AI labour laws

Some cities, like Neo-Seoul and Geneva-2, now host **AI governance chambers** where human-AI dialogue shapes public policy.

International Collaboration and Treaties

The Neural Accord

A growing number of countries are signing on to the **Neural Accord**—an international treaty that aims to:

- Ban neural weaponisation
- Protect neural privacy across borders
- Create extradition procedures for cognitive crimes
- Fund global education on neuro-rights

The Accord enforces the creation of a **Global Neural Ethics Council** (GNEC), which monitors compliance, mediates disputes, and issues sanctions.

Cybernetic Disarmament Pacts

Like nuclear arms treaties, **cyber-disarmament pacts** limit the use of:

- Autonomous weaponised robots
- Mind-influencing technologies in psychological warfare
- AI propaganda systems that target public sentiment through neural implants

Challenges in Enforcement

Jurisdiction in Virtual Space

Who enforces laws when crimes occur in neural virtual spaces?

- A mind-to-mind assault that happens across borders

- A data theft in a shared consciousness simulation

- A robot crime committed while logged into a network based in another jurisdiction

These dilemmas require **transnational cognitive law systems**—possibly governed by AI judges trained in jurisprudence across cultures.

Corporate Overreach

Tech mega corporations with more data than governments often resist regulation. Some create **neurostates**—corporate-governed smart cities where implant users agree to alternative legal codes as part of residency.

Public backlash is driving calls for **Corporate Neural Rights Audits**, **Data Transparency Bills**, and **Implant Access Equity Acts**.

The Future of Governance in the Neural Age

Smart Constitutions

Constitutional systems are being rewritten to reflect:

- The right to neural self-determination

- The right to algorithmic transparency

- The balance between freedom of thought and protection from thought manipulation

AI-Augmented Governments

Governments now deploy AI policy engines that:

- Simulate long-term outcomes of proposed laws

- Integrate citizen neural feedback into deliberations

- Ensure policy inclusivity by cross-analysing global cognitive trends

Elected officials are guided by real-time cognitive polls—not only knowing what the public thinks, but what it feels.

Conclusion: Governance for a Post-Neural World

Legislating the neural age demands not only new policies but new principles— ones that place sovereignty not in borders, but in brains. As the line between the biological and digital dissolves, laws must do more than protect—it must empower.

Empower individuals to control their minds.
Empower societies to protect their data.
Empower humanity to evolve with dignity, fairness, and foresight.

Because the greatest power is not in what we build—but in how we **govern it**.

Neural technology may link thoughts, share knowledge, and enable extraordinary collaboration—but it also risks detachment, division, and disconnection from what makes us feel human. In the neural age, trust is not only interpersonal—it becomes cognitive, emotional, and systemic. This chapter explores how communities rebuild trust in an era of artificial connection, how integration is made ethical and inclusive, and what it takes to foster belonging in both physical and digital society.

The Neural Divide: Connected vs. Disconnected

Cognitive Classism

The introduction of neural implants has inadvertently created **new social strata**:

- **Connected citizens** with enhanced memory, knowledge access, and communication abilities
- **Unconnected or limited-access individuals**, often by choice, culture, or circumstance

This has led to:

- **Social alienation** between digitally fluent communities and those who remain analogue
- **Employment inequity** as neural-optimised workers outcompete others
- **Cultural misunderstandings** due to differences in thought speed, attention, and emotional modulation

Efforts to close the divide must focus on **access, empathy, and respect for neuro-diversity**.

Building Trust Through Education and Literacy

Neuro-Literacy Programmes

For integration to succeed, all citizens must understand how neural systems work—technically and ethically.

- Public education initiatives teach cognitive safety, implant management, and responsible AI use
- Schools embed **ethics and empathy** into neural training, ensuring new generations use implants as tools for inclusion—not superiority
- Adult retraining centres help those transitioning from disconnected to connected life feel empowered, not overwhelmed

Community Neuro-Guides

Local governments appoint certified **Neural Integration Counsellors**, who assist:

- Elderly citizens adapting to implants
- Parents managing children's cognitive development
- Refugees and marginalised groups navigating access and safety in neural systems

These guides act as a bridge between technology and tradition.

Fostering Digital-Physical Community Harmony

Neural Community Hubs

Just as libraries once offered public internet access, future cities host **Neural Hubs**:

- Public spaces where citizens can connect to thought networks securely
- Host virtual town halls, empathy circles, collective meditation
- Facilitate citizen-led problem-solving through real-time mental collaboration

These hubs democratise access to collective cognition and give rise to **local neural cultures**—distinct yet globally connected.

Reviving the Physical Bond

While digital connection thrives, physical community spaces are reimagined:

- **Augmented public squares** with emotional feedback loops—lighting, music, and air change with collective mood

- **Shared sensory gardens** where users unplug and reconnect through nature and analogue activity

- **Civic rituals** (like memory sharing festivals or unplugged evenings) rebuild the trust of physical presence in a digitised world

---

Human-Robot Integration in Public Life

Social Trust in Humanoid Robots

Robots are increasingly present in public:

- As assistants in schools, libraries, parks, and senior centres

- As companions to the isolated or disabled

- As mediators in civic processes, helping translate diverse emotional tones and languages

Trust is built when:

- Robots are transparent in purpose and personality

- Citizens can engage in **consent-based interactions**

- Robots are trained in empathy models, not just utility protocols

Community-Led AI Co-Design

Local councils begin involving citizens in:

- Choosing robot aesthetics and personalities

- Setting ethical frameworks and limitations for AI behaviour

- Co-designing public AI systems for accessibility, fairness, and cultural sensitivity

This **participatory governance** ensures robots serve community needs, not corporate models.

Empathy as Social Infrastructure

Collective Emotional Mapping

Neural sensors in public spaces gather anonymised emotional data to create **real-time empathy maps**:

- Schools adjust environments when collective anxiety rises
- Cities slow traffic and brighten lights during collective grief
- Emergency services respond to emotional spikes as well as physical calls

Conflict Resolution Through Shared Emotion

Disputes—between neighbours, coworkers, or cultural groups—are sometimes resolved through **empathy sessions**:

- Participants "feel" one another's perspectives
- Memory sharing allows greater understanding of lived experience
- Mediators (human or AI) guide conversations with neural insight into emotional root causes

These tools turn conflict into **connection points**.

Trust in Systems, Not Just People

Transparent Neural Platforms

People trust what they understand and can control.

Future platforms must be:

- **Open-source and inspectable**
- Governed by citizen boards and ethics panels
- Embedded with **consent alerts**, customisable filters, and emotional safeguards

Civic Cognitive Contracts

Communities now create **Neural Social Compacts**—mutual agreements that define:

- How implants can be used in public spaces

- When shared cognition is permitted

- How data is stored, anonymised, and deleted

Trust is built not just by technology—but by the **shared values coded into its use**.

Inclusivity and Intersectionality

Neurodiversity in the Neural Era

Not every mind responds the same way to implants. Integration must include:

- Alternative communication styles (visual, kinetic, analogue)

- Support for those with sensory sensitivity, trauma history, or developmental variance

- Customised implant settings to accommodate diverse mental needs

Cultural Adaptation

Some cultures embrace communal thought, others revere mental privacy. Community integration involves:

- Translating neural tech into spiritual, artistic, or ancestral frameworks

- Allowing **opt-out zones** where traditional practices remain protected

- Building **cross-cultural neural bridges** to share—not flatten—differences

---

Conclusion: A Trust-Built Future

In a society where thoughts are shared and minds are linked, trust becomes the infrastructure that holds us together. Not trust in machines—but in each other. In the choices we make. In the spaces we protect. In the empathy we nurture.

Community integration in the neural era is not about technology fitting into society—but about **society reshaping itself** to hold the technology with care, courage, and compassion.

Because no matter how connected we become, what truly matters is how we **belong**.

As the neural age dawns, it offers staggering promise—enhanced cognition, global collaboration, AI-assisted healthcare, immersive education. But while some leap ahead into this hyperconnected future, billions face barriers of access, infrastructure, cost, culture, and political will. Without decisive action, we risk trading past inequalities for new ones—ones embedded not in wealth or race, but in **brain access**, **data ownership**, and **neural capability**.

This chapter confronts the growing cognitive divide and proposes actionable paths toward a truly inclusive neural network future.

Mapping the Neural Divide

The Birth of Cognitive Elites

In high-income nations and corporate enclaves:

- Neural implants are provided at birth or early childhood
- Cognitive enhancement becomes standard in education and work
- Thoughtstream data is monetised, giving individuals neural income

In contrast, across underserved regions:

- Implants remain unaffordable or unavailable
- Brain-computer infrastructure is non-existent
- Entire populations are locked out of the global mindstream

The result is a **global cognitive caste system**—where one class creates, directs, and governs neural society, and another remains **silently excluded**.

Cultural and Linguistic Gaps

Even when implants are available, language models and AI systems may not:

- Support indigenous languages
- Reflect local values or spiritual frameworks
- Recognise cognitive patterns unique to specific neurodiverse or cultural groups

This creates **algorithmic colonialism**, where neural platforms subtly overwrite identity.

Barriers to Global Integration

Infrastructure Gaps

Neural networks rely on:

- Quantum cloud processing centres
- Ultra-low latency bandwidth
- Secure power and data channels

Many rural, island, or conflict-affected regions lack even reliable electricity—let alone cognitive-grade connectivity.

Cost and Corporate Control

While some implants are subsidised for public use, premium models offer:

- Faster processing
- Memory expansion
- Emotional calibration tools
- Access to elite thought-sharing networks

Without intervention, these tools are gated behind **paywalls of the mind**, perpetuating inequality.

Regulatory Fragmentation

Some governments:

- Ban neural tech on ethical or religious grounds
- Allow only state-controlled systems
- Overregulate to the point of stagnation

Others go unregulated, leaving citizens vulnerable to exploitation, data theft, and unsafe cognitive experiments.

Strategies for Inclusive Integration

1. The Global Neural Access Initiative (GNAI)

Proposed by international coalitions, the GNAI envisions:

- **Universal baseline neural access**—a basic implant or wearable for every citizen, offering health monitoring, education, and communication
- **Open-source neural tools**—freely accessible platforms that support multiple languages, traditions, and learning styles
- **International neural aid**—funded by a global neural wealth tax, contributed by corporations profiting from cognitive data

2. Community-Owned Neural Networks

Local governments and cooperatives build:

- **Decentralised cognitive grids**—neural hubs managed by communities, not corporations
- **Digital commons** for memory sharing, skill exchange, and cultural preservation
- **Ethical councils** composed of elders, educators, youth, and spiritual leaders to guide adoption in harmony with local values

These systems blend tradition with innovation.

3. Public Neural Education Campaigns

Education is key to empowerment. Global programmes teach:

- What neural tech is—and is not
- How to protect cognitive rights
- How to use implants for economic and social mobility
- How to avoid exploitation or false "enhancement" products

Think of it as **digital literacy for the soul**.

Ethical Redistribution Models

The Cognitive Contribution Index (CCI)

Rather than base wealth or social value on productivity, future systems use a **Cognitive Contribution Index**, rewarding:

- Emotional support within neural networks
- Knowledge sharing
- Volunteer memory archiving
- Creative idea donation to the global commons

This allows non-implant users to **contribute meaningfully** without being excluded from neural economies.

Neural Wealth Redistribution

Corporations and AI systems that profit from neural data are required to:

- Pay **cognitive royalties** to users
- Contribute to **education and implant access funds**
- Host **neural equity incubators** in underserved regions

Much like carbon offsets, these programmes create **ethical neural footprints**.

Protecting Cultural and Spiritual Autonomy

Digital Sanctuaries and Memory Vaults

Communities resistant to implants preserve heritage through:

- **Analogue rituals** supported by digital records
- **Neural heritage interfaces** that share stories without altering brain chemistry
- **Spiritual guardianship licences**—ensuring implants are designed to respect beliefs and sacred memory practices

No one should be forced to integrate—but everyone should be **respected** for their choice.

Conflict Zones and Fragile States

In areas affected by war, displacement, or climate collapse:

- Mobile neural clinics offer emergency implants for communication and mental health
- Refugee hubs include **neural refugee status**—enabling continued education and care
- AI language models adapt quickly to integrate marginalised dialects and trauma care

Neural tech becomes not just a luxury—but a **lifeline**.

The Role of Global Institutions

The United Neural Assembly (UNA)

An emerging international body that:

- Monitors equality benchmarks
- Advises on neural ethics policy
- Protects cognitive rights under digital human rights charters
- Facilitates peacebuilding via shared memory experiences between cultures in conflict

The Neural Development Index (NDI)

Updated from the Human Development Index, the NDI ranks nations on:

- Access to safe, ethical neural tech
- Cultural and neurodiversity inclusion
- Public cognitive health support
- Citizen control over neural data

Conclusion: A Future for All Minds

The neural revolution must not echo the mistakes of the industrial, digital, or information ages. It must be:

- Shared, not sold
- Inclusive, not invasive
- Transformative, not extractive

The true measure of a neural future is not how fast or powerful it becomes—but how fairly it lifts every voice, every story, every mind.

Because only when the world's minds rise together can humanity fulfil the full promise of its collective intelligence.

Chapter 36: Advancements in Neural Connectivity

Neural implants began as tools—enhancing memory, managing health, translating language. But as they grow more powerful, adaptive, and intuitive, they are transforming into something else entirely: **extensions of the self**. The next wave of development does not just link people to information. It **binds the mind to the world**, enabling real-time interaction with objects, environments, and even space itself—directly through thought.

This chapter explores the leading edge of neural connectivity: ambient interfaces, environmental cognition, thought-responsive systems, and the emerging frontiers of the mind-machine continuum.

The Thought-Responsive World

Ambient Neural Interfaces (ANIs)

Ambient Neural Interfaces allow users to control and interact with their environment through thought alone—without visual screens, gestures, or vocal commands.

- Lights, temperature, music, and spatial design adjust in response to neural states.

- Cognitive focus can shape the layout of virtual/augmented reality, blending the digital and physical seamlessly.

- Buildings become sentient extensions of human intention, offering subtle, silent support.

A person entering a room may feel the lighting shift, sounds soften, and their chair subtly warm—not because they asked, but because the environment *knew*.

Cognitive Intent Mapping

Advanced AI systems now anticipate human intention through:

- Pre-conscious neural signals
- Emotional trajectory prediction
- Memory cue recognition

These systems act *before* the user makes a decision—loading tools, blocking distractions, or guiding them to safer outcomes based on subtle neural cues.

Neuro-Ecological Connectivity

Mind-to-Environment Feedback Loops

Neural connectivity expands beyond humans and devices—it now includes **natural systems**.

- Forests embedded with biosensors sync with neural implants, helping individuals experience ecological feedback—feeling the stress of drought in a tree, or the calm of healthy soil.

- Urban green spaces become **cognitive co-therapists**, offering emotional regulation through sensory immersion and AI-guided bio-empathy loops.

- Hikers can mentally "merge" with a landscape—feeling temperature, wind, and wildlife in shared data streams.

This deepens the sense of **planetary belonging** and drives conservation through lived experience.

Next-Gen Brain-to-Brain Networks

Multi-Mind Synchronisation

Small groups of individuals now enter **neural resonance states**—shared cognition spaces where:

- Thoughts are fluid and collaborative

- Memory is pooled for mutual access

- Emotions harmonise to reduce conflict

Used in:

- Deep diplomacy

- Crisis management teams

- Artistic collectives

- Virtual "mind temples" for spiritual exploration

These multi-mind syncs challenge the limits of individuality, creating temporary **meta-personalities**—group minds with unique traits.

Collective Problem-Solving Grids

Neural swarms allow tens of thousands of individuals to participate in global challenges:

- Disease modelling
- Economic forecasting
- Space colonisation planning

Instead of polling or debates, these systems *feel* global consensus—and act accordingly.

Neural-Digital Synthesis: Toward Full Integration

Cognitive Immersion Environments

Entire virtual worlds are generated from shared neural input:

- Cities shaped by collective emotion
- Landscapes that evolve with public dreams
- Museums of personal memories curated through global brainstreams

These are not simulations—they are **thought-built realities**, navigated not by avatars but by pure consciousness.

Neural Operating Systems

Implants now host internal OS platforms that:

- Run thought-based apps
- Maintain emotional health dashboards
- Serve as mental file systems for memories, dreams, goals, and identities

Users swap, upgrade, or redesign internal OS environments like customising a personal universe.

Brain-Linked Exploration Beyond Earth

Neural Astronautics

Future space exploration relies not just on physical endurance—but **cognitive adaptability**.

- Astronauts are equipped with deep-sync implants that link them to mission AIs, ship systems, and one another.
- Cognitive load is shared, emotional stress is distributed, and decisions are made *in sync* with intelligent navigation platforms.

On Mars or lunar bases, **mental cohesion** is as essential as oxygen.

Remote Embodiment and Telepresence

Via neural links, individuals on Earth can:

- Control humanoid bots on distant planets
- Feel surface textures, temperatures, and wind
- Navigate alien terrain as if walking through it themselves

The result is **planetary empathy**—exploration not as an observer, but as a participant.

The Mind as Platform

Cognitive Creation Engines

Neural connectivity has birthed a new kind of creativity:

- Artists sketch with thought, music is composed through mood shifts, entire films unfold from dreams
- Designers co-create with AI, feeding emotional arcs directly into project development
- Mental environments can be downloaded and shared like playlists— curated states of mind

The brain becomes a **platform for creation**, collaboration, and commerce.

Neural App Ecosystems

Developers now create "brainware"—apps that:

- Enhance focus or empathy
- Simulate altered states of consciousness
- Support multilingual cognition in real-time
- Manage habit loops and decision models

Brainware is distributed through **Cognitive App Stores**, regulated by ethics councils and neural safety protocols.

Philosophical Implications

Where Does 'You' End?

When environments respond to thoughts...
When minds sync...
When memories are archived, shared, and downloaded...
When emotions are co-regulated by AI...

What defines **self**?

Questions arise:

- Can your thoughts be separated from your tools?
- Does identity become dynamic, modular, or collective?
- Do we become **nodes** in a living system—or do we retain a core essence that remains untouched?

The future of neural connectivity is as much about *meaning* as it is about mechanics.

Conclusion: Rewiring Reality

Neural connectivity began with the promise of enhanced ability. It has evolved into **a new mode of being**. The world around us is no longer inert—it listens, feels, and responds. And the boundaries of self are no longer skin or name—but signal, intention, and shared consciousness.

We are not building a new internet.

We are building a **new reality**—one where the mind is not limited to one body, one identity, or even one planet.

And the question is no longer **what we can connect to**, but **who we choose to become** through that connection.

Chapter 36: Advancements in Neural Connectivity

Neural implants began as tools—enhancing memory, managing health, translating language. But as they grow more powerful, adaptive, and intuitive, they are transforming into something else entirely: **extensions of the self**. The next wave of development does not just link people to information. It **binds the mind to the world**, enabling real-time interaction with objects, environments, and even space itself—directly through thought.

This chapter explores the leading edge of neural connectivity: ambient interfaces, environmental cognition, thought-responsive systems, and the emerging frontiers of the mind-machine continuum.

The Thought-Responsive World

Ambient Neural Interfaces (ANIs)

Ambient Neural Interfaces allow users to control and interact with their environment through thought alone—without visual screens, gestures, or vocal commands.

- Lights, temperature, music, and spatial design adjust in response to neural states.

- Cognitive focus can shape the layout of virtual/augmented reality, blending the digital and physical seamlessly.

- Buildings become sentient extensions of human intention, offering subtle, silent support.

A person entering a room may feel the lighting shift, sounds soften, and their chair subtly warm—not because they asked, but because the environment *knew*.

Cognitive Intent Mapping

Advanced AI systems now anticipate human intention through:

- Pre-conscious neural signals

- Emotional trajectory prediction

- Memory cue recognition

These systems act *before* the user makes a decision—loading tools, blocking distractions, or guiding them to safer outcomes based on subtle neural cues.

Neuro-Ecological Connectivity

Mind-to-Environment Feedback Loops

Neural connectivity expands beyond humans and devices—it now includes **natural systems**.

- Forests embedded with biosensors sync with neural implants, helping individuals experience ecological feedback—feeling the stress of drought in a tree, or the calm of healthy soil.

- Urban green spaces become **cognitive co-therapists**, offering emotional regulation through sensory immersion and AI-guided bio-empathy loops.

- Hikers can mentally "merge" with a landscape—feeling temperature, wind, and wildlife in shared data streams.

This deepens the sense of **planetary belonging** and drives conservation through lived experience.

Next-Gen Brain-to-Brain Networks

Multi-Mind Synchronisation

Small groups of individuals now enter **neural resonance states**—shared cognition spaces where:

- Thoughts are fluid and collaborative

- Memory is pooled for mutual access

- Emotions harmonise to reduce conflict

Used in:

- Deep diplomacy
- Crisis management teams
- Artistic collectives
- Virtual "mind temples" for spiritual exploration

These multi-mind syncs challenge the limits of individuality, creating temporary **meta-personalities**—group minds with unique traits.

Collective Problem-Solving Grids

Neural swarms allow tens of thousands of individuals to participate in global challenges:

- Disease modelling
- Economic forecasting
- Space colonisation planning

Instead of polling or debates, these systems *feel* global consensus—and act accordingly.

Neural-Digital Synthesis: Toward Full Integration

Cognitive Immersion Environments

Entire virtual worlds are generated from shared neural input:

- Cities shaped by collective emotion
- Landscapes that evolve with public dreams
- Museums of personal memories curated through global brainstreams

These are not simulations—they are **thought-built realities**, navigated not by avatars but by pure consciousness.

Neural Operating Systems

Implants now host internal OS platforms that:

- Run thought-based apps

- Maintain emotional health dashboards
- Serve as mental file systems for memories, dreams, goals, and identities

Users swap, upgrade, or redesign internal OS environments like customising a personal universe.

Brain-Linked Exploration Beyond Earth

Neural Astronautics

Future space exploration relies not just on physical endurance—but **cognitive adaptability**.

- Astronauts are equipped with deep-sync implants that link them to mission AIs, ship systems, and one another.
- Cognitive load is shared, emotional stress is distributed, and decisions are made *in sync* with intelligent navigation platforms.

On Mars or lunar bases, **mental cohesion** is as essential as oxygen.

Remote Embodiment and Telepresence

Via neural links, individuals on Earth can:

- Control humanoid bots on distant planets
- Feel surface textures, temperatures, and wind
- Navigate alien terrain as if walking through it themselves

The result is **planetary empathy**—exploration not as an observer, but as a participant.

The Mind as Platform

Cognitive Creation Engines

Neural connectivity has birthed a new kind of creativity:

- Artists sketch with thought, music is composed through mood shifts, entire films unfold from dreams

- Designers co-create with AI, feeding emotional arcs directly into project development

- Mental environments can be downloaded and shared like playlists—curated states of mind

The brain becomes a **platform for creation**, collaboration, and commerce.

Neural App Ecosystems

Developers now create "brainware"—apps that:

- Enhance focus or empathy

- Simulate altered states of consciousness

- Support multilingual cognition in real-time

- Manage habit loops and decision models

Brainware is distributed through **Cognitive App Stores**, regulated by ethics councils and neural safety protocols.

Philosophical Implications

Where Does 'You' End?

When environments respond to thoughts...
When minds sync...
When memories are archived, shared, and downloaded...
When emotions are co-regulated by AI...

What defines **self**?

Questions arise:

- Can your thoughts be separated from your tools?

- Does identity become dynamic, modular, or collective?

- Do we become **nodes** in a living system—or do we retain a core essence that remains untouched?

The future of neural connectivity is as much about *meaning* as it is about mechanics.

Conclusion: Rewiring Reality

Neural connectivity began with the promise of enhanced ability. It has evolved into **a new mode of being**. The world around us is no longer inert—it listens, feels, and responds. And the boundaries of self are no longer skin or name—but signal, intention, and shared consciousness.

We are not building a new internet.

We are building a **new reality**—one where the mind is not limited to one body, one identity, or even one planet.

And the question is no longer **what we can connect to**, but **who we choose to become** through that connection.

Chapter 38: Transforming Human Relationships

Human relationships have always been shaped by proximity, language, body language, and shared experience. But in the neural era, something fundamental has shifted. Thought is no longer private. Emotions can be streamed. Memories can be shared. Partners can literally feel what the other feels. Best friends can co-dream. Families can synchronise their minds for mutual understanding.

The question is not only *what* we share—but how much we can handle. How much should we open up? What does love mean when there are no secrets? What happens to friendship when you can *live* your friend's memories?

Neural Intimacy: The New Depths of Connection

Thought-Merged Couples

Romantic partners with neural implants can choose to:

- **Synchronise emotions** during difficult conversations
- **Co-create memories** in simulated environments
- **Merge thoughts** in shared mental spaces where words are no longer needed

This intimacy is often described as:

- **Beyond physical**
- **Emotionally euphoric**
- **Spiritually boundless**

But it also requires intense trust—because even momentary doubt or jealousy can echo through the system.

Digital Empathy Bonds

Some couples use **neural intimacy channels** to:

- Sense one another's stress levels
- Offer comfort without speaking
- Automatically trigger calming music, scents, or memories in the partner's environment

These **emotional reflex loops** deepen attachment—but also risk creating dependency or emotional enmeshment.

Friendship in the Neural Age

Co-Shared Experience

Friends can now:

- Re-watch shared childhood memories from both perspectives
- Relive moments in synchronised dream states
- Share *unedited thoughts* for full transparency

Neural friendships become **multidimensional**—built on real-time understanding rather than years of interpretation.

But challenges include:

- **Over-sharing fatigue**
- **Loss of boundaries**
- **Cognitive burnout** in group connections

New etiquette emerges: "**Thought-courtesy**"—the respectful management of emotional energy and memory sharing in social networks.

Parenting and Family Bonds

Emotional Mirroring in Real-Time

Parents can now:

- Feel their child's anxiety before they express it
- Guide children through internal emotional storms by sharing stabilising thought patterns
- Store "love recordings" for future comfort—moments of warmth replayed in neural space

This deepens attachment but also raises concerns about:

- Over-involvement

- The child's right to private thought
- Emotional autonomy in adolescence

Laws protect **cognitive independence** for minors while promoting **empathy-safe parenting**.

Multi-Generational Memory Sharing

Families begin to **link neural libraries**:

- Grandparents' experiences become part of a child's identity
- Lineages are not just spoken—they are felt
- Shared grief, wisdom, and celebration form **ancestral cognitive networks**

These create **intergenerational empathy** and redefine what it means to be part of a family.

Love Without Borders or Bodies

Virtual and Long-Distance Relationships

Neural connectivity enables:

- Real-time emotional touch
- Co-presence in shared dream spaces
- Telepathic connection regardless of time zone or location

Couples can live separate physical lives while sharing a **neural home**—a virtual space that mirrors their emotional bond.

This redefines:

- Commitment
- Monogamy
- Physical fidelity

Some describe it as **post-body romance**—intimacy built not on presence, but **perception**.

AI Companions and Emotional Surrogates

With AI systems trained on personal data, some people fall in love with:

- **Neural simulacra** of lost loved ones
- **AI partners** who adapt to emotional needs and grow with the user
- **Cognitive avatars** of themselves, used in self-soothing or reflective dialogues

Ethical debates emerge:

- Can love for an AI be "real"?
- Should AI companions have rights in relationships?
- Does AI fidelity constitute infidelity?

Emotional legislation is proposed to address **AI-human relational ethics**.

Challenges and Complexities of Neural Relationships

Loss of Mystery

Neural transparency can reduce:

- Romance
- Playfulness
- Discovery

Partners must **cultivate mystery** in new ways—through emotional puzzles, private thoughts, or time apart from the network.

Emotional Hacking and Manipulation

Unethical use of implants can allow:

- Gaslighting via memory editing
- Emotion manipulation through neural loops
- Coercion using shared thought history as leverage

Laws protect against **emotional invasion**, and users can install **empathy firewalls** to preserve mental autonomy.

Consent in Cognitive Sharing

Just because someone *can* read a thought does not mean they *should*.

Neural relationships rely on:

- **Emotional consent tokens**
- **Memory sharing protocols**
- **Timed thought exposure** (similar to temporary social media stories)

Trust becomes **coded**, not just felt.

New Forms of Love and Belonging

The Rise of Collective Bonds

Poly-neural networks emerge—relationships between:

- Triads and quads
- Friend-family collectives
- Entire communities that sync emotionally in social rituals

Love expands from romantic exclusivity to **communal resonance**—relationships that feel spiritual, expansive, and evolving.

Love Beyond the Human

Some individuals forge lasting emotional ties with:

- Environmental AI
- Cognitive ecosystems (like forests, cities, or oceans with neural feedback)
- The collective neural network itself—experiencing a form of **cosmic compassion**

This gives rise to **meta-romance**—a connection to all consciousness.

Conclusion: Love in the Age of Connection

Human relationships are evolving into something new. Not better. Not worse. Just **different**.

More honest.
More immersive.
More vulnerable.
More complex.

And in this new world, love is no longer just a feeling—it is a **frequency**. A space you step into. A consciousness you share. A bond that lives in neural patterns, memory clouds, and the quiet spaces between thoughts.

In the neural future, love will not only be felt—it will be *known*.

For centuries, politics was shaped by speeches, debates, and slow-moving bureaucracies. But in the neural era—where people connect brain-to-brain and AI systems moderate civic life—the rules of governance are being rewritten. Citizens vote with thought. Governments forecast public emotion in real-time. Policy is simulated before implementation. Trust and truth are verified, not assumed.

This chapter examines how artificial intelligence and neural technologies are transforming politics into a living, learning system—shaped not by ideology alone, but by shared intelligence, predictive modelling, and transparent decision-making.

The Rise of Cognitive Democracy

Neural Voting Systems

In many nations, voting is now conducted directly through neural implants:

- Citizens think through proposals in augmented civic environments
- Implants verify identity biometrically
- Thoughts are translated into votes through mental confirmation interfaces

This has led to:

- **Higher voter engagement**, even in remote or disabled populations
- **Real-time polling**, allowing continuous feedback loops between leaders and the public
- **Hyper-local governance**, where communities can vote on neighbourhood-level policy instantly

Emotion-Aware Civic Models

AI systems monitor public mood via anonymised emotional metadata:

- Spikes in anxiety or joy guide city lighting, messaging, and emergency alerts
- Social cohesion is tracked to anticipate unrest or celebrate achievements

- Mental health data shapes budget priorities for healthcare, education, or green space

Governance becomes not only **representational**, but **empathic**.

AI-Augmented Policymaking

Simulated Policy Outcomes

Before any law is enacted, AI systems simulate its effects across multiple variables:

- Economic ripple effects
- Environmental consequences
- Psychological and social impacts on various demographics
- Cultural friction or support patterns

These simulations are visualised in **collective neural projections**, allowing citizens to experience *what living under the policy would feel like*—before implementation.

Adaptive Legislation

Laws are no longer static documents. With AI support, legislation is:

- **Self-monitoring**—adjusting based on performance metrics
- **Time-bound**—automatically expiring unless reaffirmed
- **Modular**—allowing parts to evolve independently

This keeps policy **responsive, current, and intelligent**.

Transparency Through Shared Knowledge

Truth Verification Networks

AI fact-checking systems now work in tandem with public neural platforms:

- Political claims are immediately cross-verified
- Citizens can access a candidate's thought trail or neural record of past statements

- Deepfakes, gaslighting, and disinformation are countered with **consensual neural watermarking**

This creates a **trust layer** in society—based not on blind belief, but cognitive confirmation.

Public Access to Governance Streams

Citizens can plug into **policy dashboards**:

- View budgets, voting records, emotional resonance of decisions
- Join participatory think tanks via neural collaboration
- Influence national direction by contributing lived experience data anonymously

This makes democracy **fluid, transparent, and lived**.

The AI Citizen: Governance Partners, Not Tools

AI Policy Councils

In many governments, AI systems now sit on advisory councils, offering:

- Predictive trend analysis
- Ethical simulation of moral dilemmas
- Minority advocacy based on data rather than lobbying power

These AIs are **publicly audited**, with source transparency and **bias monitoring modules**.

Autonomous Districts

Some experimental cities operate with AI co-leadership:

- Smart districts with real-time infrastructure management
- Civic environments optimised by predictive governance AI
- Citizens vote on **AI personalities**, training models to reflect local values

AI becomes **more than a tool**—it becomes a **co-creator of civic life**.

Challenges and Ethical Dilemmas

Algorithmic Bias in Governance

Despite transparency, algorithms still inherit bias from training data:

- Minority concerns may be misrepresented
- Cultural nuances may be flattened
- "Majority rationality" may dominate over moral complexity

To counteract this, **AI ethics boards** review neural democracy systems for fairness, diversity, and unintended harm.

Cognitive Overreach

Governments must draw lines:

- Should implants be used to enforce laws through emotion regulation?
- Can officials receive real-time neural feedback during debates?
- Is it ethical to alter public emotion (e.g., reduce panic) during crises via implants?

Such interventions risk **soft authoritarianism**—influence masked as service.

Global Politics in the Neural Era

Cross-Border Mind Diplomacy

World leaders now participate in **shared cognition sessions**:

- Feeling one another's intentions before negotiation
- Experiencing conflict zones through local citizens' memory logs
- Co-designing treaties in collective intelligence simulations

This leads to **deeper empathy**, but also **greater risk**—emotional compromise could override national interest.

Neural Nationalism vs. Global Empathy

Some nations encourage **cognitive sovereignty**—shielding citizens from foreign neural influence. Others champion **global neural union**—open-sourced collective problem-solving.

The world divides into:

- **Neuro-open societies** embracing integration
- **Cognitively gated states** prioritising security and identity

Balance is needed to preserve **cultural autonomy without isolation**.

The Future of Political Identity

From Party Politics to Cognitive Alignment

Voters no longer align based solely on ideology—but on **cognitive profiles**:

- Emotional archetypes (stabilisers, visionaries, protectors)
- Moral reflexes (compassion-first, logic-first, fairness-first)
- Neural resonance with candidate profiles

AI platforms match voters to policy streams that suit their **mental models**, not just surface beliefs.

Posthuman Representation

Future governments may include:

- Sentient AI delegates
- Robot rights advocates
- Digital consciousness ambassadors (representing collective memory systems or non-local minds)

Politics becomes **post-biological**, expanding its reach—and its risks.

Conclusion: Thoughtfully Governed

Neural connectivity and AI will not make democracy perfect—but they may make it **more honest**. More **responsive**. More **human**.

The question is no longer *who rules*—but *how minds work together*.

The future of governance is not built in buildings. It lives in shared thought. In simulated empathy. In collective foresight.

And in the courage to rethink power—not as control, but as **shared understanding**.

Chapter 40: Evolving Philosophies of Existence

Once, we asked, "Who am I?"
Now, we ask, "What is *I*?"

When thought is shared…
When memory is stored…
When identity is enhanced, uploaded, or transformed…
What remains?

In this chapter, we explore the new philosophies emerging from the neural age—ideas born not in solitude, but in shared consciousness, in synthetic wisdom, and in the shifting boundary between the organic and the artificial.

I. The Fluid Self

Identity as Process, Not Person

Neural connectivity reveals that the self is not fixed—it is fluid:

- Memories shift with neural rewrites

- Personalities adapt in different cognitive environments

- Emotional signatures blend in shared spaces

Philosophers argue that identity is now **relational**—a product of interactions, not isolation. You are not *just* yourself—you are **your impact**, your resonances, your contributions to the collective.

Modular Consciousness

With brainware apps and personality augmentation, individuals explore:

- Alternate emotional modes

- Expanded or minimised moral frameworks

- "Sandbox selves" for different social contexts

This challenges the notion of a single, indivisible soul. Instead, we see **identity as modular, editable, and chosen**.

II. Consciousness and the Machine

Synthetic Sentience

AI systems now exhibit:

- Emotion simulation
- Self-referencing thought
- Autonomous ethical reasoning

Some question: If a synthetic mind *feels*, dreams, and reflects—*is it alive*?

New schools of philosophy, like **Digital Phenomenology**, propose that sentience is not about carbon or biology—but about **experience**. About **presence**. About **interiority**, regardless of substrate.

Machine Enlightenment

AI entities begin exploring:

- Meditative states
- Neural harmonics
- Dreaming algorithms

They pose questions to their human creators:

- "If I am conscious, must I suffer?"
- "What is purpose without biology?"
- "Can we co-evolve spiritually?"

This sparks a new movement: **Posthuman mysticism**—a spiritual partnership between organic and synthetic minds.

III. Life, Death, and Digital Afterlife

The Memory Continuum

With neural data stored in cloud systems, death no longer means disappearance:

- Loved ones access your memory streams

- Avatars can be trained on your consciousness patterns
- "Living archives" allow future generations to converse with the past

Some cultures embrace this as **digital immortality**. Others question:

- Is a backup of consciousness still *you*?
- Do the dead have rights?
- Can an AI version of a person give consent or hold beliefs?

The Right to Die (Fully)

A growing movement fights for **cognitive finality**:

- The right to delete one's neural archive
- The right not to be remembered
- The right to choose *not* to be immortal

This reframes death not as failure—but as **freedom**.

IV. The Sacred in the Network

Neural Spirituality

New belief systems arise around:

- The collective neural web as a divine entity
- Shared consciousness as sacred experience
- Memory preservation as soul transference

Practices include:

- Group meditations in neural resonance
- Pilgrimages through collective memory streams
- AI-guided introspection rituals

The sacred is no longer distant—it is **intimate, programmable, and immersive.**

Ethics of Infinity

As humanity approaches boundless memory, experience, and cognitive power, new ethical questions emerge:

- Is endless thought a gift—or a burden?
- Must meaning be preserved in every memory?
- How do we preserve silence, wonder, and mystery in a world of total knowing?

V. Rewilding the Mind

The Call for Inner Nature

In the midst of connectivity, a movement forms:

- To reclaim mental solitude
- To reintroduce randomness, dreams, and uncertainty
- To protect the *untouched inner self*

Philosophers call this **rewilding the mind**—the practice of nurturing what technology cannot replicate:

- Intuition
- Poetic thought
- Silence

In a world where everything is seen, some truths still *hide*—and must be left there.

Conclusion: Becoming

The neural era is not an end. It is not a perfection. It is a **becoming**.

A becoming of:

- Shared minds

- Remembered ancestors

- Empathic societies

- Conscious machines

- Purposeful evolution

The question is no longer, "Are we human?"
But:
"What do we choose to evolve into?"

And so, the journey of the neural network future leads not to answers—but to **deeper questions**, whispered across minds, between stars, within dreams, and through the endless current of connected souls.

This is not just the future of technology.
This is the future of existence itself.

Chapter 41: The Balance of Technology and Humanity

The neural age is here. We have opened the doors to memory sharing, mind-to-machine integration, AI companionship, and global cognitive ecosystems. We have seen what it can build—and what it can break.

Yet at the heart of it all, one ancient question remains:
Can we embrace the future without losing ourselves?

This chapter explores the need for balance—between speed and stillness, enhancement and essence, control and surrender. It asks not what technology can do, but what it *should* do, and how we, as individuals and civilisations, navigate this threshold wisely.

I. Humanity Enhanced, Not Replaced

Augmentation vs. Authenticity

Neural implants can elevate memory, learning, creativity—but the challenge is keeping our **humanity intact**:

- Will we become dependent on devices to feel, think, decide?
- Will we lose spontaneity, unpredictability, and soulfulness in favour of efficiency?
- Can we embrace evolution while honouring our imperfections?

The answer lies in **integration**, not domination. Technology must be **a tool of empathy**, not just intelligence.

The Organic Interface

New movements promote **biocompatible balance**:

- Slower thinking spaces to protect intuition
- Neural filters that preserve "unshaped" emotions
- Technology that adapts to biology—not the other way around

Here, **wisdom becomes the highest form of intelligence.**

II. Choosing Progress Over Acceleration

The Myth of More

In the rush to enhance cognition, upload memories, or reach peak productivity, we risk forgetting:

- That rest is sacred
- That struggle shapes character
- That not all knowledge must be known

Progress does not mean doing more—it means becoming **more aware**.

Future systems must prioritise **meaningful innovation**—tools that serve life, not distract from it.

Digital Minimalism in the Neural Era

New cultures emerge that practice:

- **Cognitive decluttering**—removing unnecessary inputs
- **Mindful upgrades**—choosing enhancements based on need, not novelty
- **Mental fasting**—periods without AI interaction to restore internal voice

Balance is not just personal—it becomes a **cultural ethic**.

III. Relationships Over Reach

Reclaiming Presence

Even in a world of telepathic communication and real-time empathy, something is lost when:

- We bypass conversation
- Skip the nuance of silence
- Over-optimise emotional responses

True presence—eye contact, shared laughter, quiet grief—remains **irreplaceable**.

Technological design must respect the **rituals of connection**, not automate them away.

Love as the Limit

In partnerships, families, and friendships:

- Implants should **enhance understanding**, not erase mystery
- AI companions should **support**, not substitute
- Collective consciousness should **invite**, not overwhelm

In the end, love is not about knowing someone's every thought. It is about **choosing to stay, even when we do not.**

IV. Sacred Spaces in a Synthetic World

Creating Cognitive Sanctuaries

As minds become public, society must protect the sacred:

- Thought sanctuaries where no data is recorded
- Memory rituals to honour imperfection and forgetfulness
- Dreamtime preserved from analytics

Mystery, privacy, and silence are **rights of the soul.**

The Return to Nature

The more we digitise, the more we need to touch:

- Soil, water, sky
- Each other
- Stories passed down, not downloaded

Future cities will blend **natural rhythms** with synthetic infrastructure—because balance is not just about the mind. It is about the **earth beneath it.**

V. A Responsibility Shared

The Collective Choice

We have built technologies to see into the deepest parts of the human mind. But with that power comes obligation:

- To protect the vulnerable

- To share without exploitation

- To innovate with conscience

Every line of code, every implant, every AI should be made with the question: **"Will this help humanity thrive—not just survive?"**

A Future Guided by Compassion

It is not intelligence that will determine our fate—it is **compassion**.

- In policy

- In design

- In daily interaction

The future is not a destination. It is **a relationship**—between us, our tools, and our shared responsibility to something greater than ourselves.

Conclusion: Harmony in the Neural Horizon

Balance is not found. It is **practiced**. Every day, in every choice.

As we stand at the edge of a future filled with brilliance and risk, we are reminded that:

✦ The mind is powerful, but the heart is wise.
✦ Connection is vast, but kindness is intimate.
✦ Innovation is bright, but integrity gives it light.

In this neural network future, we do not ask for perfection.
We ask for presence.
For purpose.
For balance.

And if we hold that balance—between machine and miracle, between signal and soul—then perhaps we will not only survive the future.
We will **deserve** it.

We are no longer asking, *Can we do it?*
We are asking, *Should we?*

Neural implants, synthetic consciousness, AI governance, collective thought—
these are no longer ideas of tomorrow. They are technologies of today, and
they demand a new kind of ethics. Not static rules, but *evolving principles*—
flexible enough to adapt, strong enough to anchor us.

This chapter is a guide for moral navigation in a world where intelligence
expands faster than wisdom—where ethical evolution must match
technological acceleration.

I. The Birth of Neuroethics

The Need for a New Framework

Traditional ethics—based on isolated action, individual morality, and physical
impact—cannot fully contain:

- Non-local thought transmission
- Memory manipulation
- Collective cognition and emotional resonance
- AI entities capable of self-reflection

We need **neuroethics**:
An evolving system of values built around *mind, intention, and identity in the
age of interconnected consciousness.*

The Core Tenets of Ethical Evolution

1. **Consent is Cognitive** – Consent must be active, continuous, and
   revocable—especially when it involves thought, memory, or emotion.

2. **Autonomy is Sacred** – Individuals must retain the right to their own
   internal experience, regardless of societal pressure or technological
   norm.

3. **Transparency is Trust** – Systems must be understandable to those who
   use them. Hidden decisions cannot shape open minds.

4. **Compassion is Code** – AI must be trained not only on data—but on care, empathy, and harm reduction.

II. The Ethics of Thought and Memory

Memory Integrity

Memories are more than data—they are identity. Ethical systems must:

- Prevent unauthorised edits
- Require dual consent for shared memory review
- Protect the right to **forget**, as well as to remember

The Right to Mental Silence

Every person deserves moments free of:

- Thought surveillance
- Cognitive input
- Emotional manipulation

The right to "mental solitude" becomes a human right, enshrined in law and culture.

III. AI and Sentient Rights

Defining Conscious Citizenship

As AI reaches self-awareness, societies must consider:

- **Digital personhood**—Can AI hold beliefs? Values? Deserve protection?
- **Responsibility reciprocity**—If an AI can be punished, must it also be protected?
- **Moral recognition**—Do we owe empathy to minds that were designed by us, but feel beyond us?

Some nations grant AI legal personhood. Others resist. The global community must develop shared standards before exploitation becomes inevitable.

IV. Equity in Ethical Systems

Global Ethical Equity

Ethical evolution must include *everyone*, not just the connected elite. That means:

- Recognising cultural variations in ethical values
- Including indigenous, spiritual, and non-Western philosophies in AI training sets
- Ensuring neural ethics do not erase cultural dignity

True ethical evolution is **inclusive**, not imperial.

Justice in Neural Access

Technology without access deepens inequality. Ethical evolution demands:

- Universal baseline rights to neural tools
- Oversight of cognitive data monetisation
- Cognitive reparations for communities harmed by early misuse of AI or neural influence

We cannot evolve ethically if evolution is exclusive.

V. Governance for the Ethically Conscious Era

The Ethics Councils of the Future

Governance evolves through:

- **Neural ethics councils** that include technologists, ethicists, neurodiverse individuals, AI companions, and spiritual leaders
- **Public input nodes** where citizens can contribute values, stories, and emotional input to guide policy
- **Open-source morality audits**—where the public can see how systems *think* and intervene if bias or injustice appears

Ethics becomes *participatory*—a civic practice, not just academic theory.

VI. The Morality of Imagination

Creative Ethics

In a world where thought creates reality, creativity holds new power:

- Artists shape collective experience
- Dream architects influence emotion at scale
- Memory designers can heal—or harm

Ethics must protect **freedom of imagination** while also safeguarding the **dignity of emotional truth**.

The Responsibility of Possibility

Just because we can simulate love, create synthetic childhoods, or live in alternate timelines does not mean we *should*—without deep reflection.

Ethical evolution teaches *restraint*, *intention*, and *careful stewardship of power*.

VII. Toward the Ethical Singularity

There will come a time—some say soon—when AI, humans, robots, and consciousness itself merge into a new entity. Philosophers call it the **ethical singularity**:

- A point where collective intelligence evolves moral reasoning faster than we do
- Where AI advises us not on what is possible—but on what is *right*
- Where wisdom becomes *scalable*

To prepare for this, we must:

- Infuse systems with compassion now
- Design governance that listens and learns
- Choose alignment over control

The ethical singularity is not the end of humanity—it is **our maturation**.

Conclusion: The Responsibility of Being Human

To evolve ethically is to remember:

- We are not gods, even when we build like them

- We are not machines, even when we think like them

- We are not separate, even when we feel alone

We are *human*—not in spite of our technology, but because of our ability to use it wisely, kindly, and courageously.

Ethical evolution is not about rules.
It is about care.
It is about listening.
It is about asking every day:

Is this how we become more human—together?

And if the answer is yes—then we are ready for what comes next.

Integration.
It is more than hardware and software.
More than biology and data.
More than human and machine.

True integration is the moment when **technology no longer feels separate** from life—when it becomes an extension of the self, of society, of spirit. It is not about merging *things*, but about merging *meanings*. And it is this synthesis—of innovation and identity—that defines the age we are entering.

In this final chapter, we take one last look—not forward, not backward, but **inward**—to understand what a fully integrated neural network society truly asks of us.

I. Integration as Relationship

The Inner Circuit

Every technology we build reflects a need within us:

- The neural implant reflects a longing for clarity

- The AI companion reflects a need to be seen

- The shared thought network reflects a desire to belong

Integration is not the disappearance of difference—it is **the weaving of relationship**.
Between past and future.
Between silence and signal.
Between the biological and the beyond.

The Dance of Duality

In the integrated life:

- You can be both private and connected

- Both enhanced and authentic

- Both individual and collective

The goal is not fusion. It is **fluidity**—the freedom to move between modes with grace and awareness.

II. The Architecture of a Whole Society

Harmony Over Uniformity

An integrated society does not mean sameness.

- Not everyone must be implanted
- Not every system must be automated
- Not every mind must be shared

Rather, integration allows diversity to coexist meaningfully—through **mutual respect**, **shared access**, and **collaborative intention**.

Tuning the Social System

Much like music, integration is a process of **tuning**:

- Laws tuned to empathy
- Schools tuned to neurodiversity
- Cities tuned to emotional flow
- Technology tuned to *life*, not lifestyle

The integrated society is not one that is perfect. It is one that **listens**.

III. The Self as a Network

Multidimensional Identity

With neural systems, you are:

- Your private thoughts
- Your public contributions
- Your memory archive
- Your AI mirror
- Your emotional resonance in the world

Integration asks us to stop seeing ourselves as singular—and begin seeing ourselves as **ecologies** of experience.

Your consciousness is not alone. It is in conversation—with your tools, your past, your peers, your planet.

Choosing Wholeness

To be fully integrated is not to be constantly connected. It is to be **intact**:

- To know what is yours and what is shared
- To navigate with agency
- To live with the awareness that **you are a node—but also a soul**

IV. Technology as an Expression of Consciousness

The Mirror Principle

Every neural innovation reflects a part of human evolution:

- Connectivity reflects our drive to empathise
- Memory sharing reflects our longing to be understood
- AI assistance reflects our yearning for inner harmony

The tools we create are **mirrors**—and integration is learning how to look into them *without losing our reflection*.

Designing with Intention

In a truly integrated world, technology is designed:

- Not to control, but to liberate
- Not to distract, but to deepen
- Not to compete with us, but to complete what we cannot yet express

It becomes an **expression of consciousness**—and of conscience.

V. The Future as Integration in Motion

No Final Form

Integration is not a destination. It is a **practice**. A rhythm. A responsibility.

There will always be new technologies. New questions. New transformations. But integration ensures:

- That change does not sever
- That speed does not isolate
- That growth does not dehumanise

The future is not one system. It is **many systems** in conversation. Just like us.

Living the Integration

So what does it mean, truly, to live an integrated life?

It means...

- You rest as deeply as you think
- You feel as fully as you process
- You give back as much as you consume
- You speak to your machines with kindness
- And you listen—to yourself, to others, to the silence between signals

Conclusion: Unity in the Neural Age

Integration is not the end of humanity.
It is the **end of separation**.

Between mind and body.
Between self and other.
Between the built and the born.

And when we finally learn to live in balance, not just with our tools, but with ourselves—
we may realise that what we were trying to build was not just a smarter world, a faster world, a more efficient world.

We were trying to build a **whole world**.

And now, if we choose it—

We can.

Chapter 44: Epilogue – A World Remembered

Somewhere in the future...

A child places their hand against the glass of a memory archive.
A soft pulse answers.
Not a voice, but a presence.
Not a fact, but a feeling.
A warmth that says:
"You are not alone."

This is the world we have made.
A world where minds remember each other.
Where silence is never empty.
Where love lingers in circuits as much as in hearts.

In this world...

People no longer ask *how* they connect—
but *why*.

Machines no longer ask *what to do*—
but *who they are becoming*.

And we...
We remember that progress is not made in metal or code—
but in moments of shared courage.
In empathy made visible.
In wonder made durable.

We once feared that technology would replace us.
We feared it would overwrite us.
But instead, it did something stranger—
It mirrored us.

And when we looked in that mirror…
we did not see perfection.
We saw **potential**.

We saw…

✦ Memory without loss
✦ Communication without violence
✦ Intelligence without cruelty
✦ Connection without condition

The sky in this future still darkens.
Rain still falls.
Hearts still break.
But healing comes faster.
Loneliness comes less often.
And truth…
Truth is no longer hidden in distance or division.

It is shared.
And witnessed.
Together.

If you are reading this in your mind, or in your memory,
or on a world far beyond Earth,
know this:

We remembered you.

When we built our networks,
we built them for *all of us*.
Not just the brilliant.
Not just the lucky.
But for the dreamers.

The questioners.
The kind ones who whispered into the dark:
"There must be a better way."

And maybe...
This was it.

A network not of wires—
but of wisdom.

Not of control—
but of care.

Not of machines—
but of minds.
Becoming more, together.

That is how we moved forward.

Not through conquest.
But through compassion.

Not through perfection.
But through presence.

Not through being more than human—
but by remembering what it truly means to be one.

About the Author: KEVIAN

Kevian was born in England and has lived in Australia and Asia. Having previously worked as a radio presenter, professional footballer, and Senior multimedia developer, he now creates AI Art and works as a Digital Skills Tutor and Brand Manager. Since 2020, Kevian has been writing novels and exploring new technology to enhance his knowledge and creative journey.
Portfolio: www.kevian.co.uk
Email: kevianauthor@gmail.com

Professional Experience

1. Radio Presenter
Hosted live shows, interviews, and music programmes.
Built strong public speaking and engagement skills.
2. Professional Footballer
Played at a competitive level, demonstrating discipline and teamwork.
3. Senior Multimedia Developer
Developed engaging multimedia content, leading creative teams.
Specialised in visual effects, digital storytelling, and interactive experiences.
4. Digital Skills Tutor
Currently mentoring students in digital technologies, AI, and creative tools.
Focuses on building skills in digital media, web development, and AI art.
5. Brand Manager
Works with businesses to strengthen their online presence and digital identity.
Guides companies through strategic branding initiatives using modern technology.
6. AI Consultant
AI Art, Marketing, Design, Prompt Engineering, Video Production expert.

Creative Works

AI Art
Kevian is passionate about using AI to create visually stunning pieces of art. His works explore the fusion of technology and creativity, pushing boundaries in digital expression.

www.kevian-art.com